chosen
to
heal

Gifted Catholics Share Stories of God's
Miraculous Healing Power

by Laura Wright

Cover painting by Brian Jekel

Immaculate Heart Press

ISBN-13: 978-0-9910864-0-5

DEDICATION

For my parents, Robert and Susan Jamison.

"Love begins at home, and it is not how much we do ... but how much love we put in that action." Blessed Mother Teresa

CONTENTS

INTRODUCTION

Sometimes the world is a scary place. Our bodies fail us, loved ones pass away, people hurt each other, and tragedy strikes unexpectedly.

That's why God gives us miraculous reminders that there is life and hope beyond this "valley of tears."

The six Catholics who I profiled in this book are well acquainted with God's wondrous handiwork here on earth. Each of them has a God-given gift of healing, and they see His miracles firsthand, almost every day.

Much like the first apostles, they have devoted their lives to healing the sick and preaching the Gospel to further the Church and bring more souls to Jesus.

You will read the dramatic story of a former mobster who converted and received the gift of healing during the 15 years he spent in prison, and another story of an 85-year-old woman who has trained priests in spiritual warfare and casts out demons in Jesus' name.

My great hope is that after you read this book you will tell your friends and neighbors — especially those who are sick — to ask Jesus for spiritual and physical healing. I wrote about gifted Catholics who live in different parts of the country so great distances wouldn't separate you from the healing prayers you may seek. If you are too ill to travel even short distances, you should consider prayerfully going to Jesus in the Eucharist or receiving the Anointing of the Sick. Many miraculous recoveries have been attributed to these two powerful sacraments.

Inside, you will hear stories of spiritual renewal, deliverance and breathtaking physical healings. Because of the extraordinary nature of many of these miracles, they are sometimes hard to believe.

But as my husband reminded me, so many fundamental teachings of our faith are miracles that by definition defy logic – God became man, He was born of a virgin, and then He rose from the dead and ascended into heaven. We also believe Jesus is truly present with us in the Eucharist at every Mass.

There seems to be little room for doubt after accepting these wondrous teachings. This does not mean that every miracle you hear about is from God or is true, but it does mean that we must continue in prayerful discernment and never lose sight of God's miraculous healing power.

I also encourage you to remember what it means to have childlike faith, because Jesus tells us in the Bible that "unless you change and become like little children, you will never enter the kingdom of heaven," (Matthew 8:3). When I was about ten years old I was praying the rosary with my cousin and my mother. Sensing our mild boredom, my mom asked us if she could pray for the Blessed Mother to appear to us. Shocked and excited, we hastily said yes. But as my mother began to pray, my cousin cried out to stop her, "No! Wait." She was slightly terrified at the thought of an apparition, because she really believed it could happen.

I'm sure God was smiling down on us that day, appreciating our full and vibrant faith, however silly it seems today.

I invite anyone who doubts in God or His miracles to spend a day in the presence of one of the individuals profiled in this book – their faith in Christ will either rattle you awake or serve as a catalyst for serious reflection about your faith life.

And while this is not a glossary of perfectly holy people, these individuals offer us two very important examples of what it means to live out our faith – they pray unceasingly and they truly believe God hears their prayers.

Ay, there's the rub – prayer. It is so dangerously easy to neglect our relationship with God, because everything else we are doing seems just slightly more urgent or interesting than praying.

But a poor prayer life creates cracks in the foundation of our faith that if left unfixed can quickly separate us from Jesus.

One individual profiled in this book said pride would have consumed him and his healing ministry if he didn't stay close to the Lord in prayer. The world's vanities and troubles can be too much for anyone to shoulder alone, and that is why God offers us His help when we pray and He reminds us of His presence with miracles.

St. Augustine of Hippo hoped that just as the miracles of Jesus' first disciples helped build the early Church, miracles of his own time would draw people to Jesus too.

He wrote in De Civitate Dei (City of God), "What do these miracles attest but the faith which proclaims that Christ rose in the flesh and ascended into heaven with the flesh?"

But St. Augustine did not always believe in the miracles of his day – he had the same doubts that persist in many of us. Early in his ministry he wrote in De Vera Religione (On the True Religion) that miracles like those recounted in the Bible had ended soon after Jesus' death, "lest the mind should always seek visible things."

St. Augustine dramatically changed his position when he personally encountered miraculous events. The saint later went on to examine, record and give publicity to these miracles.

In City of God St. Augustine writes about the miracle of Innocentia, a respected citizen and holy woman who doctors diagnosed with advanced breast cancer.

St. Augustine wrote that "She turned for help to God alone, in prayer."

In a dream she was told to wait in the church for the first woman who came out after receiving Baptism, and to ask this woman to make the sign of the cross over her breast.

Innocentia followed these instructions and was miraculously healed. St. Augustine later discovered she had not told anyone about her healing, and urged her to share her story.

"I was indignant that so astounding a miracle, performed in so important a city, and on a person far from obscure, should have been kept a secret like this; and I thought it right to admonish her and to speak to her with some sharpness on the matter," he wrote.

St. Augustine's change of heart toward miracles reminds us to continually seek and proclaim the truth. If we receive a miracle, we should share this news with others for the glory of God, and if we hear about a miracle, we should not immediately dismiss its authenticity.

While this attitude of faith seems like it should come naturally for Catholics who have a rich history of mystics and miracles to draw from, this isn't always the case. We put these mystical saints and older, approved miracles in an "amazing things that happened in the past" box. Transitioning to understanding the supernatural in our own lives is difficult, but very important if we want to grow in our relationship with Jesus. How will God speak to us if we refuse to listen to the Holy Spirit moving in our hearts? This awareness of God's Presence stems from an openness to the supernatural that is always guided and modified by the Church and Her precepts.

A priest profiled in this book, Father Dan Leary, speaking at a women's night of recollection with healing prayers, explained the importance of the Church's healing ministry saying he joined four other priests and a bishop in praying for more than 400 people at a nearby Catholic school. "I wanted to frame that because healing is part of the culture of the Church, and it is a natural charism of the priest. When you don't want prayer it makes me sad. I say, 'Man, they must not be sick or know anyone suffering, because this is a viable option for them.'"

The Church has always reached out to help the sick, suffering and possessed. Even Jesus and His apostles spent a large part of their ministry casting out demons and healing people. Today, the Church acknowledges the validity of healing charisms and prescribes the Rite of Exorcism and the Sacrament of the Anointing of the Sick to assist in healing. Unfortunately, the laity and sometimes priests are under educated on the reality of possession and the true healing power of God through the sacraments and prayers.

Father Richard McAlear, another priest profiled in this book, said Catholics sometimes feel uncomfortable with prayers for deliverance and healing, because we associate these activities with Pentecostals, who hold boisterous tent revivals.

"We are not good at that. We had to develop something that was more Catholic. The charismatic renewal within the Church was about laying hands on people and praying quietly. It is much more incarnational than the approach taken by Pentecostals," he said.

The Vatican document on healing – Instruction on Prayers for Healing – is very clear about the way people with a healing charism should conduct their gatherings.

"Anything resembling hysteria, artificiality, theatricality or sensationalism, above all on the part of those who are in charge of such gatherings, must not take place," the document reads.

It also confirms that prayer for healing has been a part of the Church's experience at every age, and that longing for happiness and a desire to be free from illness is "deeply rooted in the human heart."

Father McAlear says some believers suffer from "Catholic Schizophrenia"– they accept their suffering, but only ask the doctor for healing, not God.

"Yes, you should unite your suffering to Christ on the Cross, but also ask for healing," he said.

The Vatican acknowledges the reality and mystery of healing charisms by referring to what St. Paul said in 1 Corinthians 12. The saint does not attribute healing charisms to any particular group – like teachers or prophets – instead, the document says, "All these [healing gifts] are activated by one and the same Spirit, Who distributes to each one individually just as the Spirit chooses."

And just as God chooses who He gifts with a healing charism, so God may also choose to grant miracles to people of different faiths, Father McAlear explains.

He paraphrased something St. Thomas Aquinas, a famous theologian and Doctor of the Church, wrote in the Summa Theologica, "We are restricted to God's laws, but God is not restricted to God's laws."

Father McAlear went on to explain, "God does whatever God wants to do," and this may or may not include granting miracles to people of different faiths.

But Father McAlear does see a serious problem when people claim to heal by harnessing heat and energy, or by applying other new age practices. These "healers" leave no room for God, the Creator of all things, including heat and energy. Instead, they slowly succumb to pride and moral relativism by claiming they are the healer. Many Catholic and Christian leaders strongly caution people against seeking out this type of healing, because it's not from God.

The Vatican issued a study – "Jesus Christ the Bearer of the Water of Life: A Christian reflection on the 'New Age'" – explaining the clear differences between new age practices and Christianity. The study presents the Gospel of John's account of Jesus' meeting with the Samaritan woman at the well as an example of how to counsel people taken in by new age "spiritual narcissism."

The study says Jesus' loving approach toward the woman at the well, "could yield a rich harvest in terms of people who may have been attracted to the water-carrier (Aquarius) but who are genuinely still seeking truth. They should be invited to listen to Jesus, who offers us not simply something that will quench our thirst today, but the hidden depths of "living water.""

This search for healing and truth – however misguided at times – cuts across all faiths and types of people. It also reminds us of two unchanging realities – people will always search for miracles, and God will always love us.

Jesus' tender love of His dear friend Lazarus demonstrates this clearly. When Lazarus was gravely ill, his sisters sent for Jesus' help, but He did not come immediately. Jesus knew that while Lazarus would die and more tears would be shed in His absence, a greater purpose would be served if He waited. Jesus arrived to a scene of terrible grief and He was so moved by it that He wept with the other mourners over his dead friend.

While Jesus knew He would go on to raise Lazarus from the dead, He demonstrated sincere empathy for our sufferings with His tears. "Jesus Wept," (John 11:35) is the shortest verse in the Bible. It powerfully reminds us that Jesus was both God and man because He responded to the loss of His dear friend with human tears. Satan, not Jesus, is the author of pain, suffering and death. And because we have free will we must ask God to give back what Satan has taken from us.

Whether we receive an instant cure, a partial cure or no cure at all, it remains a miracle to have the absolute love of an omniscient God.

I pray you will be amazed by His love in the stories recounted in this book, and continue to look forward to the final healing we will all receive in Heaven.

Blessed Mother, pray for us. St. Philomena, pray for us. St. Michael the Archangel, pray for us. St. Martin de Porres, pray for us. St. Therese, pray for us.

Sacred Heart of Jesus have mercy on us.

1 | DOMINGO SETIEN

"Come to me, all you who are weary and burdened, and I will give you rest." Matthew 11:28

Doctors told Maria Teresa Garza, a young mother, she had three months to live.

She had already undergone several surgeries, and radiation treatments in hopes of curing the ovarian cancer that had metastasized in her body. Pain was her constant companion, along with the prescription drugs she used to dull the agony. Sitting caused her extreme discomfort, and keeping food down was a fight she lost often. But Maria Teresa may have suffered the most when the haunting thought of leaving behind her husband and two young children surfaced in her mind.

Back at home, a few days after her third surgery her pain was particularly excruciating. Her husband, Salvador Garza, called Domingo Setien. He asked Domingo to say a simple prayer for his dying wife.

Domingo, who had not yet begun his work in the healing ministry, told him not to worry about his wife. He was going to pray for her, and she would be ok.

Domingo marveled at the words that came out of his own mouth. He questioned his boldness. Why had he told the husband of a dying woman she was going to recover?

Having graduated from a Catholic college with degrees in philosophy and theology, Domingo was trained to understand God in terms of clear reasoning and sound logic. But in the realm of miracles – supernatural occurrences that defy logic – he was less experienced. Still, he felt led by the Spirit in his prayers for Maria's recovery.

RESTORED

The next morning Maria Teresa was in her kitchen cooking huevos rancheros. It was the first time in six months that she was able to enjoy eating. Shut away in her medicine cabinet were the pain killers. She didn't need them anymore – God had granted her a miracle.

The following day Maria Teresa went back to her oncologists. They had difficulty believing their findings. She was cancer-free. And Maria Teresa remained cancer-free since that day in 1974. She is now 83, and she thanks God every day for the gift of life.

BEGINNINGS

Domingo's healing ministry began to take shape after Maria Teresa's miracle. People began asking him for prayers that God oftentimes answered in wondrous ways. Rosie, his wife of 57 years, said when the miracles started happening she would have been skeptical if they hadn't been so tangible.

The wheel chair bound could now walk, the infertile could have children, and tumors vanished.

LOVE STORY

In the entryway to the Setien's modest San Antonio home, there hangs a picture of the couple on their wedding day. Many years later and grayer, now in their eighties, they look surprisingly the same – smiling and joyful.

In between laughs, Domingo and Rosie share their love story. They met in Domingo's cousin's grocery store where he worked as a bagger, and she lived next door. When Rosie checked out at the register, Domingo wrote his number and a note on the box of Corn Flakes she bought that said, "call me."

Rosie called, and five children and nearly six decades later they still enjoy listening to each other talk. They also share the heavy load of the healing ministry. A striped yellow notebook always sits next to the phone with the names and numbers of hundreds of people that call for healing prayers.

They call from all over the world. Logged in the notebook are their countries and prayer requests. Domingo prays for each person, and he calls back those facing emergency situations. He believes most people learn about his ministry on the internet, or by word of mouth, but always with the help of the Holy Spirit.

WALKING ON WATER

Sometimes the Holy Spirit's involvement is undeniable. Such was the case when Domingo's phone rang one night at

11 p.m.

A woman from Louisiana was on the line calling about her husband in the intensive care unit. He had a diastolic blood pressure reading of 40, and unless he received an operation his chances of survival were slim. The doctors couldn't begin the procedure until he had reached a blood pressure level of 70.

Still hazy-eyed from sleep, Domingo made his way to the make-shift altar in his home. A painting of Jesus walking on water is the most prominent artwork there – a constant reminder of God's power to do the miraculous.

"Lord, I need your help," he humbly prayed. As he continued in prayer the woman watched her husband's blood pressure. It began to rise steadily. The doctor – called in to watch the climbing blood pressure – started shouting out numbers. "He is at 50 now. Sixty. Sixty-five. He is at 70." The operation began immediately.

SHROUDED IN MYSTERY

There can be no doubt that Jesus still grants miracles today, Domingo says. But why did God choose him for this great task? He has no answer. Others speculate.

Domingo grew up in Tamaulipas, Mexico in the small town of Juamave. By example, his parents instilled in him the virtues of living modestly and charitably.

His parents owned the town's oldest restaurant and his mother would invite anyone who was poor and hungry to come and eat there for free. No one went hungry in Juamave, Domingo boasts.

Today, Domingo carries on a tradition of charity with the

proceeds he raises from the healing ministry. None of the money benefits him directly. One third goes to the Church, one third supports the efforts of the healing ministry, and the last third is reserved for the poor in Mexico. Domingo personally makes the trip to his native country once a year around Christmastime to distribute the money among the needy.

Further proof of his modest lifestyle is found in his possessions. Domingo's ivy-covered, small brick house doesn't make a bold declaration of wealth. Neither does the white Honda parked in the driveway out front.

Inside, there are no fancy trappings, if one excludes the abundant religious artwork. The homes in the surrounding neighborhood are equally modest in appearance. A subtle irony exists for some homes that have bars on their windows, but crosses on their doors.

Living humbly helps Domingo do God's healing work. He believes that with out humility, God will not work through him. But it can be challenging to remain humble when barraged with a multitude of requests for healing, and media interviews.

To combat the almost natural path to pride, Domingo "checks in with God" every night by examining his conscience. He also prays the Liturgy of the Hours in the morning and evening, and spends time with God throughout the day.

Domingo readily admits that he is far from perfect, making it all the more mysterious and humbling that God would choose him for such a noble purpose.

BY THE THOUSANDS

Domingo doesn't ask why he was chosen for this task, he just submits to God's will and trusts. That trust has led him to effectively lead healing services with thousands of people.

Following a string of newspaper stories about Domingo in the San Antonio Express Newspaper in 2003, crowds began to swell at his healing services. For about eight weeks in the winter of that year about 1000 to 2000 people were coming to find healing.

A U.S. Marshall on Domingo's prayer team gave him advice on how to control the large crowds. Anyone who wanted a prayer had to remain seated. Domingo allowed 800 people into the Church at a time. Two police officers were stationed outside the Church and the city of San Antonio positioned 10 more to guide traffic along the already busy roads near the parish.

St. Margaret Mary church – Domingo's home parish for nearly 50 years – hosted the services. The parish remained at full capacity for the entire eight weeks – spreading the Gospel message to lapsed Catholics, Christians, atheists and people of different faiths.

The days were long, sometimes starting early and lasting into the evening. Although it was tiring, God gave Domingo the strength he needed. Over each person he made the sign of the cross and prayed while gently touching their forehead. If someone had a critical illness Domingo would spend more time praying with them.

Domingo recalls a man who suffered from severe back pain searching for a healing at one of the eight crowded services. He had been to several healers, and nothing had worked. He told Domingo he was skeptical, but he was willing to try anything if it might ease the constant pain.

During each service, before Domingo prays over people individually, he listens to the Holy Spirit and receives a gift of knowledge. He knows how many people are being healed in each seating section of the church, and in faith, he calls out the numbers. He asks people to raise their hands if they have received a healing. The Holy Spirit has not been wrong yet, Domingo says.

Such was the case for the skeptic. He was one of 8 people who raised their hand that day. His back pain had disappeared. At the next service he came back and brought 16 people with him.

FRIENDS IN HIGH PLACES

A close friend of Domingo, San Antonio Archbishop Emeritus Patrick Flores, also attended one of the eight healing services. The archbishop has expressed continued support for Domingo's ministry over the years – referring people to him for spiritual and physical healing.

In a letter of recommendation the archbishop praised Domingo saying, "Mr. Setien has helped me in many, many ways ... teaching people who need help, who need the Word of God, who need material blessings. Mr. Setien has been a teacher of the Scriptures, has been involved in spiritual and physical healing and does it in a very mature and sound way."

His support however, doesn't mean the Church has verified and approved the miracles people believe they have received through Domingo. The Church maintains a rigorous approval process that can take decades or longer, and many miracles are never submitted to the Church for approval.

For one young boy possessed by an evil spirit, Domingo's healing touch made all the difference. The nine-year-old-boy would wake up in the middle of the night filled with rage. He frequently tried to attack his parents while he was in this state. The terrified family took extra precautions – putting locks on doors and setting alarm clocks to check on him throughout the night. After seeking the help of doctors, psychiatrists and several priests, they were finally directed to Domingo by the archbishop.

Domingo recalls his first meeting with James (name changed to protect anonymity) – he had red, blood-shot eyes. He was tired, stubborn and abnormally strong. After sprinkling Holy Water on him, Domingo bent his head and prayed for deliverance. The boy's resistance dissolved immediately, and he started weeping uncontrollably. James and Domingo walked around the house together arm-in-arm, talking. His parents watched on in shocked awe. The answer to their many prayers had come in an instant.

Following a recommendation of the archbishop, the boy and his family attended Domingo's healing services every Tuesday for a year afterward, and he has had no further problems. Today, James is a young adult considering the priesthood.

In 2003, San Antonio's WOAI News Channel 4 featured Domingo in a story about the boy's deliverance. The story was leaked to the press by an insider in the archbishop's office. The news station superimposed the words "the exorcist" on Domingo's shirt. Domingo took issue with the identification of the boy and the use of the word exorcist in the story. Archbishop Flores also disapproved of the news story, saying the word exorcism has been hijacked by Hollywood, and this type of sensationalism should be avoided.

Exorcism is a rite of the Church consisting of specific prayers and rituals. Priests maintain the exclusive responsibility to use this rite to cast out demons, and many diocese have an exorcist appointed by the bishop. Lay Catholics do not use the Church's rite of exorcism – instead they deliver people using their own set of methods that may be equally effective.

Son of the Church

Domingo has long experienced support for his ministry from the archbishop, who has called on him for help numerous times.

When the archbishop needed to raise a large sum of money, he came to Domingo and his healing ministry team for prayer. Three days later, he received the donation he needed.

Another time, Archbishop Flores came to Domingo for help in deciding the name of a newly built parish. He invited Domingo over for breakfast to brainstorm, and during their meal they received a providential phone call. Pope John Paul II was on the line. The archbishop told the pontiff, "I'm here with my friend who is helping me name a new church."

The pope didn't hesitate – he offered a name for the parish immediately. Today, in Poteet, Texas sits St. Peter the Fisherman Parish. Domingo's task was complete.

The archbishop also recommends Domingo to friends who need healing. Domingo remembers a house visit he made on behalf of the archbishop. He was greeted by an unfriendly dog, and a husband clearly affected by grief. He seemed disconnected – he was slow to answer the door, and slower to introduce Domingo to his wife. She had been on life support for the past six months, and her prospects of recovering were bleak.

Finally, after much stalling, he took Domingo to his wife's room. It was in perfect order, but a feeling of sadness permeated it. Domingo prayed over the sick woman and told the couple they would see a big change.

The next week, at the same time, Domingo went back. The woman was sitting up and disconnected from her life support. Another week passed, and Domingo visited her again. She was sitting in the kitchen, and the couple seemed happier – they had gained hope back. Three days later, to Domingo's astonishment, the woman passed away.

A friend had given her "miracle water" from Mexico that wasn't from an approved Catholic source. It was laden with bacteria that her fragile immune system couldn't handle.

This experience further shaped Domingo's understanding of authority in relation to miracles. It is ultimately God's decision to grant a miracle, and take a miracle away. People may also jeopardize their chances of receiving a healing when they put something else before God, like the questionable "miracle water."

Spiritual healing must also take place before physical healing can happen effectively, he said. Oftentimes people will come to him holding grudges, and they haven't learned how to forgive. This is why the first prayer Domingo says on behalf of the people at his healing services is for spiritual cleanliness.

SKEPTICS AND BELIEVERS

Ironically though, sometimes people who have no faith at all experience a miracle. In the Gospel, Jesus effectively brought people to believe in Him through miracles, and it remains this way today. In the name of Jesus, Domingo has brought dozens of lapsed Catholics and atheists back to the Church. He attributes every miracle to God's unfathomable mercy and love for us.

Four years ago, Sylvia Madrigal came to Domingo as a skeptic, suffering the ravages of a a severe illness. Sylvia, in her fifties, suffered from lupus, diabetes, and numerous complications. She was wheel-chair bound and relied on an oxygen tank to breath. The doctors gave her six months to live.

Sylvia had been in the hospital for several weeks and in the wheel chair for a month before a friend took her to Domingo's healing service. She was hesitant, but the unbearable pain was an excellent motivator. That night Sylvia didn't receive a healing, but she was moved by the service enough to come back a second and third time. She had seen the broken people, just like her, shuffle into the pews – following hope, however dim it seemed.

God saw her there, searching for Him and a way out of her misery. During the third healing service, Sylvia received a miracle. She felt a warmness flood through her body as

Domingo prayed over her. But this explanation falls short. She grasped for the adjectives to explain her experience, but couldn't. It's like trying to explain God.

Sylvia quietly left the healing service and headed home. Slowly, she took off the oxygen mask that had sustained her. It didn't serve a purpose anymore, because she was breathing regularly. She then abandoned her wheel chair and walked across the room.

Her husband and three children stood speechless, watching the event unfold. Doctors who had predicted her impending death were equally baffled by her recovery. Sylvia continued to suffer from her disease, but God lightened her burden and gave her four more treasured years with her family before she was finally called home in January, 2013.

Before her death, Sylvia said her supernatural experience also helped her grow in faith and love of the Lord. "It really has changed my life," she said.

Sylvia recruited Domingo to offer a healing service at her home parish once a month. He also hosts a weekly healing service at St. Gerard Catholic Church in San Antonio, his home parish for the past nine years.

Domingo doesn't have an end in mind for his healing ministry. As long as God is willing to show His love to the world through miracles, Domingo will remain His humble servant.

For more information on Domingo and his healing ministry go to www.setienhealingministries.org.

Domingo Setien and his wife, Rosie, pose together in a recent photo. Domingo and Rosie have five children together, and they have been married nearly 60 years. (Photo Courtesy of Domingo Setien)

Sylvia Madrigal and her husband, George, enjoy a trip outside together before her healing. Sylvia suffered from lupus and diabetes and was confined to her wheel chair. (Photo Courtesy of George Madrigal)

2 | TOM NAEMI

"And my speech and my message were not in plausible words of wisdom, but in demonstration of the Spirit and of power." 1 Corinthians 2:4

Rage settled in Tom Naemi's soul as he brewed over the ugly rivalry threatening his family's Detroit grocery store.

It had begun with a small deception. His competition had planted a mole to work in Tom's supermarket. She intentionally gave bad service and told loyal customers to shop somewhere else. When the deception finally came to light, Tom ran to the rival store and angrily confronted them. People were screaming in the aisles as the episode escalated into violence. Tom left the store shouting prophetic words, "You don't know who you are messing with. I'll be your worst nightmare."

And since that day, Tom and his enemies lived like mobsters – Tom fire bombed their store several times, they hired hit men to take Tom out, and he chased them with guns down Detroit's notorious Seven Mile strip. Finally, Tom decided it was time to end it.

On a clear and quiet night, he loaded a truck with 575 gallons of gasoline and 12 pipe bombs and drove it toward his competitors store. This time he would blow up their store beyond repair. This time he would finish them. But he didn't want anyone to get hurt. He knew no one would be working there that night.

Armed with an uzi, 13 bullet clips, and an alibi, Tom felt ready. He pulled into an abandoned warehouse near the grocery store, lit the three-minute fuse, and the truck lit up like an angry furnace. Tom was shocked – the fumes inside the truck had caught fire immediately. He would have to act quickly.

He jumped into the burning truck and drove it toward the grocery store, but it exploded prematurely. He dove out of the truck, the right side of his face had already melted off, and his hands and feet were burned to the bone.

The truck stopped 20 feet in front of the grocery store, and then gave up. It sat there – covered in furious orange and yellow flames – a living memorial to Tom's angry past, and a foreshadowing of his future life set ablaze by the Holy Spirit.

MOBSTER DIARIES

His wife and four children had begged him to stop before this. On her knees, his wife pleaded with him to end the bitter war he had with his competitors.

But how could he? He was too entrenched.

Growing up in a rough neighborhood in Detroit and burdened with a fast temper, Tom's destiny seemed unalterably linked to this fiery violence.

The city streets weren't kind to Tom – he quickly learned to fight while making deliveries for his uncle's party shop. Anger and ambition, he believed, were necessary for survival.

By 23, Tom was a prosperous man, and by 24 he lost it all by over-investing. He promised himself he would do whatever it took to earn it back. Running from the fire he started to destroy his competition – skin sloughing off his face – he was fulfilling that promise.

BURNS AND BARS

Tom ran from the scene – distant thoughts buzzed through his head, and the searing pain he would later feel had not yet come into focus.

His friend cautiously opened her door to Tom after the fire, because she didn't recognize his burnt face. "Who is it?" she kept asking, before Tom reassured her that it was really him.

"How bad is it?" he asked.

Her expression was grave – he needed to get to a hospital. Tom had a friend blow up a car for him so he had an excuse for the burns when he arrived, but they quickly figured out the real cause.

Doctors told Tom he had suffered third degree burns over 47 percent of his body. He underwent four surgeries and a grueling healing process that kept authorities from putting him in prison.

Months later he fled to Iraq, his home country, to keep from being put in jail, but came back because he missed his wife and four children.

They met secretly in California, but he was discovered by authorities and fled once again to Iraq. Several months passed before Tom decided to return and give himself up. His lawyer said he would get at most eight years, maybe five if he was lucky.

But the judge rocked his plans for a short prison stay – she sentenced Tom to 60 to 90 years.

He walked into Jackson Prison with 12 other men. A former drug dealer confided in him that he was scared, and Tom reassured him that he would cut anyone's head off who messed with him inside those walls.

Tom spent 5 years in close custody – permitted outside for only a few hours a day. After that, the judge dropped him to level 2 security and reduced his sentence to 15 to 40 years in prison.

He was later sent to Lapeer Prison where some convicts read the Bible and sang worship songs in the jail yard. They were '"idiots," Tom decided.

But you had to fill the day with activities in prison – so Tom decided to go to Catholic service. After all, he was an altar boy as a child, and in the tiniest corner of his soul remained the seed of faith. God was still calling him.

SKETCHES OF FAITH

When Tom lived in Iraq as a boy, his father told him never to let anyone blaspheme Jesus or the Blessed Mother, and if they did, he should beat them up.

Living as a Catholic in a Muslim country was challenging, so when Tom was 11 years old his family immigrated to the United States and settled in Detroit. Tom's father and family could now worship freely.

Ironically, only now that Tom was locked up in prison did he begin rediscovering the importance of this freedom that his father had won for him.

One of his first memories at the Catholic prison service is of Deacon Ed kneeling before the Eucharist for almost 10 minutes.

"This guy is overdoing it. He is showing off. We all know this is Jesus, so get up already," he thought.

Afterward, Deacon Ed Bauroph asked Tom "How is your walk with the Lord?"

Tom responded cooly, "Well, my walk with the Lord is good. I just want to go home because I have a score to settle with some people. I made a mistake in not finishing it."

Deacon Ed admonished him saying, "Tom! What's wrong with you? You are a Christian. Where is your forgiveness? You have to change your life, and ask Jesus to intervene for you."

Deacon Ed's words had cut surprisingly deep. Every day Tom asked Jesus to help him forgive. Years went by and Tom noticed the hatred toward his enemies had abated and happiness started to grow in its place.

One night Tom was watching a preacher on television who asked, "Do you have a relationship with Jesus, or are you just a church goer?"

Tom thought, "Yes. This man is right. I never really made Jesus my friend." So that night, he sat up on his bunk and prayed honestly and openly with the Lord. He confessed that he had made a mess of things on his own, and he needed Jesus to take it from there.

"Lord, I give you my whole life," he prayed.

THE JESUS DREAMS

A few nights later Tom began having dreams of the Lord. In his first dream he was preaching divine healing to a skeptical crowd. He woke up confused – why would God want him, of all people, to preach on divine healing? What did he know about that?

Nothing.

But the dreams kept coming. He was walking into a beautiful white mansion with four pillars. As he came into the living room he saw a picture of the Sacred Heart of Jesus.

Admiring it, Tom said, "Lord, You truly are handsome."

And then Jesus' eyes moved. He spoke to Tom saying, "Do not be afraid. Your cousin Steve has pain on his left side. I want you to tell him to drink a little bit of red wine every night for a little while and he will be healed."

Jesus repeated this to Tom a second and a third time.

When Tom woke up he was reluctant to call his cousin – he would think Tom had gone crazy, but he called anyway.

"Are you sick Steve?"

He was. So Tom delivered the message. His cousin was healed shortly thereafter.

In another dream Tom saw a couple familiar to him arguing. They were considering divorce. God said to Tom, "Tell them I hate divorce. Tell them to look deep into their hearts and find the love that is still there. The same love they had when they got married."

But the Lord warned Tom they wouldn't believe him, so He gave Tom a secret to share with them about their life before they were married.

Tom called up the couple and asked them if they were considering divorce.

"How did you know?" his friend responded. He told them about his dream, and when they didn't believe him, he told them the secret that God had entrusted with him to secure their faith. Stunned and touched that the Lord had spoken through Tom, they promised to begin working on their relationship.

His next dream was of a friend who had left his wife for another woman. He was sitting in a recliner, drinking, and depressed. Jesus said to Tom, "Tell him he must repent now."

Tom called him and asked, "How are you doing?"

"I'm good," he said.

"No you're not," Tom replied. "You are living with this woman who is not your wife. You are living in sin. This woman is abusing you and taking all your money. I saw you. You were miserable with a bottle in your hands. You need to change your life and come to Jesus," he said.

Tom went on to have several more dreams of Jesus – conversing with Him, and telling Him which parts of the Bible he most loved to read. He also prayed for an intimate knowledge of Scripture and it was given to him. Tom can quote nearly any verse of Scripture from memory.

Around this time the Catholic prison ministry began a seven-week-long life in the Spirit seminar that Tom participated in. At the end of the seminar Tom confessed to a priest a grave sin that had held him back from fully serving the Lord – pride.

Then volunteers prayed over the inmates to receive the gifts of the Holy Spirit. They asked Tom how he felt, but he said nothing had changed.

COME HOLY SPIRIT

The next morning Tom woke up and went about his normal prison routine – he slapped peanut butter and honey on toast and poured some hot water for coffee.

He put on his ear phones, turned on the news, and finished making his sandwich.

He was only halfheartedly listening to the reporter who said the word "God." But at that moment, when "God" was uttered, a strong wind accompanied by a loud buzzing sound rushed into Tom's cell. It felt as if it went right through him and his body temperature began to rise dramatically.

Tom called out to his cellmate and friend, "Ray! Jesus is in the house!"

Ray Akrawi, still groggy from waking up said, "Tom, you have lost your mind. What is the matter with you?"

Tom responded by walking over to Ray and asking him if he could pray over his foot and ankle. Ray – standing over 6 feet tall, and made of mostly muscle – had often complained of his ankle that he twisted playing baseball. Even though he was younger than Tom, he took the bottom bunk because of his condition.

Tom put his hands about a foot away from Ray's face and began to pray to the Lord. Ray immediately felt warmth radiating from Tom.

The next day Ray played basketball. His foot and ankle were healed.

ON THE OUTSIDE

On Nov. 15, 2005 Tom was released from prison after more than 15 years. In many ways his life was forever altered by his stay in jail. During his time there he and his wife divorced, and Tom received an annulment. His four children had grown up, and although he stays in close contact with them, he missed much of their childhood. For Tom, speaking of his family remains a tender subject.

Before his release Tom seriously considered joining the priesthood, but was met with skepticism from Church officials who didn't take the ex-convict seriously. This grieved Tom, but he has since dedicated himself to serving the Lord as a lay person – especially by using his healing charism to glorify God.

DAN AND NANCY BIANCHI
"He was moved with pity for them" Matthew 9:36

Dan Bianchi can't stop telling people about the healing he received from Jesus through Tom's prayer's. Twenty-three years ago Dan fell from a corn elevator, fracturing his pelvis. He also broke his ankle twice over the years.

These injuries left him with severe arthritis in his joints and many sleepless nights. The sheet on his bed was completely worn away in the spot where his ankle rubbed against it. Dan stifled the extreme discomfort with a daily regimen of pain pills.

Eventually Dan's pain grew worse. He could no longer bike to work, or take walks with his wife, Nancy. As a Ford factory worker he stood on his feet all day long, and wore tight knee braces for support.

After working one eight-hour night shift he came home and cried in front of his wife. He wasn't sure he could keep working because of the pain, but retirement benefits were only a few months away.

With nine children – the youngest of whom was nine – he felt the heavy responsibility of providing for his family.

On March 18, 2011, both he and his wife attended a free class on healing at Sacred Heart Major Seminary in Detroit.

After class, Dan was in line for Confession when his wife ordered him into the room where Tom was praying over people. Dan, skeptical, reluctantly went to be prayed over.

As Tom and a few other men prayed over his legs, Dan felt a jolting pain shoot out of his right knee.

"They made it worse!" he thought. Then Dan felt pins and needles from his waste down. He left the healing service quietly, mulling over what had just happened.

"Am I just imagining this renewed strength in my legs?" he thought.

But he wasn't. The following day he helped move his son's heavy furniture up and down stairs, and the day after that he walked to the river with his wife. For an entire week Dan felt as though his legs – and especially his knees – had cool, moist air blowing on them.

Dan no longer needed to retire early, or even take pain medication. God had healed him.

God also healed Dan's wife, Nancy. Her faith suffered because she resented God for allowing her husband to get sick.

These feelings changed when Jesus healed Dan. Nancy is grateful to God for healing her husband, but even more for healing her heart. Nancy told everyone about her husband's miracle and the undeniable power and presence of God in her life.

Since then, Nancy has twice invited Tom to come to her parish. During both visits, people spilled out of the pews, in large part because of Nancy's zeal to share her story, and spread the message of God's love.

Baby Christian Youssif
"Pray without ceasing" Thessalonians 5:16

Mrossia Youssif knew something was wrong when her baby, Christian, began crying continuously and battled countless colds, high fevers and ear infections.

She took her son to the doctor numerous times, desperate for answers, but he always sent her back home, with a recommendation that she stop worrying so much. He told her that as long as the baby was eating and growing, nothing was wrong.

But Christian's health continued to decline. A month after a doctor's visit Mrossia noticed one of Christian's eyes started drooping and looking to only one side.

Soon after this observation Christian accidentally fell off the bed and Mrossia took him to the emergency room. He wouldn't stop crying, but the doctor examined him and found nothing wrong. He bit his lip, that's all, the doctor said. Mrossia pleaded for him to at least take an x-ray. The results were baffling. Christian's heart was not on the left side of his body like it is on most people, but on the right.

A heart specialist told her later that this explained his weak immune system, but that his condition was not life threatening.

Another month and a half went by and Christian's illness continued to worsen. His legs were weak and he couldn't bear weight on them. Mrossia knew her son was sicker than the doctors believed so she asked St. Charbel, a mystical Lebanese hermit, to help her discover the real cause of his suffering.

The saint provided her an answer the following Sunday. Christian had not stopped crying for three days, and Mrossia decided to take him back to the emergency room.

But this time, when the doctor came in and told her there was nothing wrong with her son, Mrossia started screaming.

"He has been on antibiotics for three months! My child can not explain himself, but I can feel it," she yelled.

The doctor told her she was behaving rudely, and was about to dismiss her when a nurse stepped in to say she had seen the child in the hospital before. She recommended that they give the baby a blood test, and the doctor agreed.

It was midnight and Mrossia was told to sit in the waiting room with her pale, sick baby – they would call her when the results came back. She asked her husband if she was hearing things when her son's name was urgently called out over the loudspeaker.

"Christian Youssif is needed in the emergency room immediately."

Before she could get up to take her son, the nurse came rushing into the waiting room.

"We have to give your son a blood transfusion or he is going to die," she said.

Mrossia reluctantly gave up her son. "Here is my child. I don't want him to die," she barely got out.

The doctor explained that Christian's hemoglobin was dangerously low. They also discovered that the earlier diagnosis about his heart had been wrong, and that he had a kidney tumor. The doctor recommended that Christian transfer to Sickkids Hospital in Toronto, a hospital specializing in the care of sick children.

As Mrossia rode in the ambulance with her son she kept praying, "You gave him to me, please don't take him from me. I named him Christian, because I wanted him to be a good Christian."

Christian's new doctor finally gave Mrossia an accurate diagnosis – Christian had neuroblastoma, a cancer found in infants and children. It started in his adrenal gland, but it had spread all over his body, and now it was stage four cancer. He had a 30 percent chance of survival.

The doctor handed her a piece of paper describing the planned treatment – first chemotherapy, then a bone marrow transplant, then more chemotherapy and possibly surgery after that.

Mrossia's heart was drowned in grief at the thought of losing her son and she cried, "Why God? Why my son? I've always been close to You."

Christian underwent the first round of chemotherapy and couldn't stop crying. Mrossia pressed the doctor to figure out what was wrong, so they took another scan and found a collection of unknown material about the size of potato next to his kidney. They thought it might be an infection so they put him on antibiotics. Christian's chances of survival looked graver than ever.

The next day, Mrossia's cousin's friend– Tom Naemi – arrived to the hospital to pray over Christian. The baby was lethargic and pale after his second round of chemotherapy and was laying down on his mother when Tom walked into the room.

To Mrossia's disbelief, her sick son immediately sat up, as if greeting Tom, and tried to jump out of her arms to reach him. When Mrossia handed Christian to Tom, the baby began playing with Tom's face.

Turning to Mrossia, Tom looked at her intently and said, "Your son will be cured. You have to believe in God and His miracles."

The following day Christian was a spectacle of hope – the collection of material the size of a potato was gone. The doctor noted in surprise that the antibiotics would not have eliminated an infection that quickly. The baby also responded exceptionally well to the chemotherapy – his tumor had decreased from 8 cm to almost 1 cm.

Christian's remaining small tumor was treated with chemotherapy, and his adrenal gland was removed as a precaution. Christian is now a happy and healthy 4 year old, and his mother remains humbly grateful to God for her son's miraculous healing, St. Charbel's aid, and Tom's intercessory prayers.

NITA SADEK
"Let not your hearts be troubled" John 14:1

Only a couple weeks after Nita Sadek delivered twins her doctor told her she had a lump in her breast.

Terrified, Nita went in for an ultrasound to rule out breast cancer. The results came back negative – she didn't have cancer, but thoughts of dying and suffering lingered in her mind. Still unsettled, Nita got a second opinion from a breast cancer surgeon who also told her she didn't have cancer.

Nita's family members were relieved, but her own fear and anxiety continued to escalate. She would wake up in the middle of the night with thoughts of dying painfully and leaving her children behind. The anxiety was crippling, and her relationships and work suffered because of it.

"I couldn't even have a normal life anymore. I was smiling and laughing with people, but in the back of my head I was thinking to myself, 'I am going to die,'" she said.

Desperate, Nita went to a psychologist who diagnosed her with severe anxiety. She introduced Nita to behavioral therapy, and encouraged her to look at pictures of breast cancer survivors who had mastectomies.

"It was making it worse, and I stopped going," she said. Nita felt like she was walking on a tight rope that could snap at any moment. Having suffered from this anxiety for two years, she wanted more than anything for her mind to stop racing, and to rest.

She told Jesus in her desperation, "If You take me right now in a car accident I would feel relief."

A short time after making this prayer a friend of Tom's came to get her hair done with Nita, a hairdresser. They began talking about Jesus, and Nita felt inspired to tell her about her anxiety. She asked Nita to let Tom pray over her, and she agreed.

It was early January 2011 when Nita first met Tom. She immediately felt comfortable with him and began crying and sharing her story. When she finished, Tom asked, "You know the devil is a liar, right?"

He then began to pray over Nita – rebuking Satan and reciting verses from the Bible.

As Tom prayed Nita felt like a weight was being lifted off of her body. She now knew that Satan was twisting her thoughts, and she had to rebuke him the next time it began.

"These thoughts still come up, but they don't control me anymore. I know how to fight it," she said. "That was almost three years ago, and now I am a different person. I completely did a turn around and I got to know Jesus on a different level. I literally had strength that you wouldn't believe."

Before this miracle, Nita was reluctant to share her faith with clients, and couldn't bring herself to put a picture of Jesus at her workstation for fear of offending someone.

"I wasn't afraid to tell them and talk to them about Jesus anymore. I told them, 'I believe Jesus can heal you. Just give it a chance.' And they would give it a chance," she said. She convinced a Jewish client suffering from cancer to let Tom pray over her.

The next day she texted Nita saying she would be interested in going again with Nita or even by herself.

Nita's love of Jesus continues to grow, and with it grows the knowledge that Christ brings healing to a broken world filled with many wounded hearts.

STEPHANIE ABBO

"Let thy tender mercies come unto me, that I may live."
Psalms 119:77

Stephanie Abbo felt physically and spiritually bankrupt before she met Tom. In 2000, she was diagnosed with acute hypothyroidism – a condition in which the thyroid gland does not produce enough thyroid hormone. Her case was so severe that her doctor marveled that she wasn't in a coma. Stephanie – then 25 years old – would need to take a replacement thyroid hormone every day for the rest of her life or she would die.

Eleven years after her diagnosis, Stephanie was going through a major personal hardship. She was a cradle Catholic who no longer practiced her faith in earnest, but her suffering reminded her to rely more on Jesus. Slowly, she began going back to church.

At St. Thomas Chaldean Catholic Church – the parish Tom belongs to – Stephanie joined a Bible study and began participating in Mass. One evening, she picked up the church bulletin and noticed a healing Mass scheduled for the next day. She told Father Frank Kalabat, the pastor there, she would come.

Even though she had second thoughts about going to Mass two days in a row, she felt a persistent urge to go and be closer to Jesus. Following the Mass, Tom prayed over her.

She remembers falling to the floor, only aware of the peace and tranquility enveloping her.

She told Tom later, "I believe in this, but I just don't believe I will be one of the ones to heal."

Tom replied, "You are healing."

"Ok," she answered skeptically.

Before the second healing Mass Stephanie attended she prayed, "Jesus, I know sometimes I sound skeptical when I pray, but I really do believe in Your miracles. Can You please heal me? Thank You, I love You, Jesus."

She paused and then added, "Jesus, my doctor says I can die if I get off this medication, but I would really like to get off this medication. If I can't, can you please reduce the dose at least."

Jesus heard Stephanie's prayer. Shortly after the second healing Mass Stephanie went to her yearly thyroid check-up. Her thyroid hormone levels had remained fairly consistent since her initial diagnosis more than 10 years earlier.

But when her latest lab results came back, the doctor called her to say he didn't understand why, but her condition had dramatically improved and he substantially reduced her thyroid medication.

Two months later – in Dec. 2011 – Stephanie went in for another check up, the doctor checked her levels, and he reduced her medication even more.

Stephanie continues to heal in many ways – her life was forever altered by the fire of the Holy Spirit burning in Tom's heart that quickly spread to her own. She now serves God by helping others – she volunteers in prison ministry; visits the sick in hospitals; writes and speaks about abortion and sacramental marriage, and prays tirelessly for her relatives and friends to find Jesus.

TOM'S MESSAGE

Tom – whose life ended in fire and began again in the fire of the Holy Spirit – prays that everyone he meets will let the Holy Spirit burn brightly in their hearts.

At the end of every healing Mass Tom reminds those who came in search of a miracle that Jesus has already healed each one of us.

He quotes Isaiah 53:5, saying, "He was wounded for our transgressions, He was bruised for our iniquities: the chastisement of our peace was upon Him; and with His stripes we are healed."

Dan Bianchi, healed of severe arthritis and joint pain through the intercessory prayers of Tom Naemi, poses with his nine children in a 2007 family photo. From top to bottom and left to right are Jeff, Joseph, John, Sarah, Michael, Christina, Katie, Dan, Nancy, Thomas and Martha. (Photo Courtesy of Dan Bianchi)

Tom Naemi (center) poses for a photo with his sons Tommy (left) and Tony inside the prison where he was incarcerated. The photo was taken in 1998. (Photo Courtesy of Tom Naemi)

3 | FATHER JOSE MANIYANGAT

"This sickness is not unto death, but for the glory of God, that the Son of God may be glorified through it," John 11:4

The tasks of the day occupied Father Jose Maniyangat's thoughts as he rode his second-hand motorcycle to a rural mission church in India, his homeland.

It was Divine Mercy Sunday, 1985, and at the bishop's request he was going to celebrate Mass for the people there.

But God had other plans for the young priest – A drunk driver leaving a local Hindu festival crashed his jeep into Father Jose head on, killing him instantly.

Father Jose immediately felt his soul leave his body and he saw his guardian angel, radiant and glowing. He also saw people crying – they were taking him to the hospital.

Then his guardian angel spoke – Father Jose was going to Heaven, and on the way he would visit hell and Purgatory.

FIRE

The images of hell are forever emblazoned on the priest's heart and mind. People were screaming and fighting – some tortured by demons – in unquenchable fire. The angel said that just one mortal sin could take a soul to hell. But the angel reassured Father Jose that no matter how many mortal sins a person committed, if they repented of those grave sins, they would not go to hell.

Father Jose was also surprised and saddened to see some priests and bishops burning in hell for misleading the faithful with bad example and false teaching.

Season of longing

After Father Jose experienced hell, his angel took him to Purgatory. As the unbearable suffering of hell began to abate, another kind of suffering – one buoyed by hope, but filled with intense longing for Jesus – was found in its place.

Here, in Purgatory, Father Jose saw seven degrees of suffering. On the deepest levels souls suffered unquenchable fire, but it was less intense than the unquenchable fire of hell, and there was no fighting. The greatest suffering for these souls was their separation from Jesus. When Father Jose spoke to the souls in purgatory, they pleaded for his prayers, and the prayers of others so they could finally rest with Jesus in heaven. In return, they promised to loyally pray for anyone who interceded for them.

The priest was also given special knowledge about the value of suffering – repentant sinners may be purified of their sins through their earthly sufferings, and avoid time in purgatory. Sinners who have not experienced hardship in this life, will experience it in the next according to God's perfect justice and mercy.

These insights line up with the strong tradition of Scripture that a great reversal awaits us in the after life. Jesus said, "But many who are first will be last, and the last will be first," (Matthew 19:30).

Joy untold

Father Jose knew his visit with the poor souls in Purgatory had ended when he began to feel overwhelming joy as he passed through a brilliant white tunnel with his angel. He heard the most beautiful, ethereal music, and he realized – this was Heaven. The Blessed Mother, St. Joseph, the saints, bishops, priests and many other souls were there, glowing and bright.

Then there was Jesus, more radiant than a thousand rising suns. He told the priest, "I want you to go back to the world. In your second life you will be an instrument of peace and healing to my people. You will walk in a foreign land and you will speak a foreign tongue. Everything is possible for you with My grace." Then the Blessed Mother told him, "Do whatever He tells you. I will help you in your ministries."

But Father Jose didn't want to leave. Peace and joy enveloped him and he couldn't tear himself away from it. He knew now – Heaven was his real home and everyone was created to reach Heaven and enjoy God forever. Why would he ever go back?

ALIVE

Pain tore through his body and he found himself alive and screaming. The nurse who was carting Father Jose to the morgue on a gurney, started shouting in fear, "The dead body is screaming! The dead body is screaming!" Terrified, she ran for the doctor.

The doctor who declared Father Jose dead upon his arrival to the hospital couldn't believe what the nurse was trying to tell him.

"How?" the doctor thought. His examination had been thorough – Father Jose bled to death. The priest's family had already been notified. But when the doctor reached the priest, his doubts vanished and he shouted, "Father is alive! It's a miracle. Take him back to the hospital."

Father Jose immediately received blood transfusions followed by multiple surgeries to repair many broken bones. For weeks, doctors worked on his lower jaw, ribs, pelvic bone, wrists, and right leg.

The healing process was grueling. After two months, Father Jose was released from the hospital. The orthopedic doctor who took care of him during his long recovery said he would never walk again. Father prayed with his family for a miracle, but a month after his release he still couldn't move.

POWER TO HEAL

One day, praying alone, the priest asked again for healing. This time the response was immediate – Father Jose felt an extraordinary pain in his pelvic area and then it disappeared completely. He heard a voice say, "You are healed. Get up and walk."

Father Jose immediately walked to the telephone to call his orthopedic doctor, a Hindu, and tell him about his miraculous recovery.

The doctor was taken aback, but what he asked Father Jose next both surprised and humbled the priest.

"Will you teach me about your Church and your God?" he asked.

Father Jose felt reaffirmed that God's plan for him was not just to heal bodies through Christ, but to heal souls. The doctor came into the Church in 1986, after Father Jose helped him learn about Christ and the Church.

This first miracle characterizes Father Jose's healing ministry perfectly. While there is no shortage of physical healings in the priest's ministry, the healings that mean the most to Father Jose are spiritual. Soon after Father Jose recovered he was assigned to a parish in Florida.

NEW LIFE

Diana King will never forget the day she met Father Jose. Catholicism was foreign to her. But her deep longing for a child, unsatisfied because of infertility, opened her heart to the idea of attending a healing Mass.

Once a liberal feminist and intellectual with degrees from Harvard and Emerson College, Diana had spent a large part of her life as an agnostic. Slowly, she became interested in Christianity. By the time she went to work for a conservative news agency, she considered herself a non-denominational Protestant. She later went on to write a popular, heart-wrenching book called "Terri's Story," about the death of Terri Schiavo, a disabled woman on life support. Terri became the subject of international controversy after her estranged husband obtained a court order to remove her feeding tube and dehydrate her to death over the strenuous objections of her parents.

While writing about Terri's tragedy Diana and her husband Don, both approaching their forties, were experiencing a personal tragedy. They couldn't conceive children, and they were doing everything in their power to alter their bleak prospects. They spent upwards of $30,000 relying on science to boost Diana's fertility – undergoing in vitro fertilization twice – only to be told by experts that Diana was simply too old and her eggs couldn't fertilize.

Diana and Don were crushed. In vitro fertilization had been anguishing – she swamped her body with hormones, put on 20 pounds, and she was emotionally exhausted.

The controversial procedure creates moral dilemmas for mothers whose eggs do fertilize properly. Many live with the haunting thought that they may never give birth to all the resulting embryos, leaving these babies to sit on ice indefinitely. And in other cases, IVF leads to selective abortions. Fertility experts typically implant more embryos into the mother than the desired number of babies in order to increase the odds for success. But if all implanted embryos survive and attach to the uterine lining, women who don't want to carry multiple babies opt to abort the excess.

When Diana finally decided to walk away from what science had to offer, a Catholic friend who she met while writing her book suggested that she attend one of Father Jose's healing Masses.

On Dec. 5, 2005, Diana and Don, a fallen-away

Catholic, attended their first healing Mass. Diana was moved by the solemnity and mystery of the Mass, and Father Jose's deep love of Christ and Our Lady. During the next six months Diana came to every healing Mass, and learned more about the Blessed Mother. She asked for Mary's intercession and strongly felt that the Blessed Mother was praying for her to conceive a child.

Diana found out she was pregnant in June. Doctors estimated that she conceived the baby on May 13, the feast of the first day of the six appearances of the Blessed Mother in Fatima. She gave birth at 42 years old to a little boy named Justin. About 3 years later, after continuing to attend healing Masses, Diana gave birth to Olivia Marie.

Today the family lives a very active faith life. Diana converted to Catholicism, and Don experienced a renewed love of the faith.

Diana looks back now and can see God's hand everywhere – leading her more closely to Him through her acceptance of His tender mother and His faithful servant, Father Jose.

In the testimony Don and Diana published on Father Jose's website they wrote

"The definition of grace is an undeserved gift from God. We'd like to introduce you to Justin ... He is our grace."

JESUS, MY FRIEND

Just down the hall from Father Jose's room is his best friend, Jesus, alive in the Blessed Sacrament in the chapel where the priest prays daily.

"I love having Jesus as my roommate," he says with a

smile.

When visitors come to see Father Jose he instructs them to go and spend time with Jesus first, then they can talk.

Father Jose cultivated his love for the Lord growing up in a small town of farmers, where his family had animals and worked the land for food. The familiar smell of curry filled their home, reminding the family to gather for mealtime and to give thanks to God for their blessings. The priest, the oldest of seven children, remembers his parents leading them in morning prayer and a family rosary in the evening.

When Father Jose was seven years old he told his parents he wanted to become a priest, and they responded with full support. They felt honored that God planted the seed of this vocation in their son's soul at such a young age.

Father Jose's lifelong dream was fulfilled when he turned 25 – he was ordained to the priesthood so he could serve God with all his heart.

At times, the priest admits to missing his family and the familiar food and culture of his homeland, but these feelings are secondary to his mission to further the Kingdom of God.

SERVANT OF THE CHURCH

St. Augustine Bishop Felipe Estevez recently moved Father Jose from St. Mary's Church in Macclenny, where he served as pastor, to St. Catherine of Siena Parish in Orange Park so he could devote himself more fully to his healing ministry. Father Jose now serves as parochial vicar at St. Catherine's, and he celebrates a monthly healing Mass on the first Saturday of each month.

On Father Jose's website he prominently posted a statement from the Diocese of St. Augustine stating, "Neither the Diocese of St. Augustine, nor any Catholic Church authorities have investigated, approved or in any way endorsed the factual or theological contents of the Father Jose story."

The Church maintains a rigorous approval process for miracles and apparitions that can span over the course of decades. Oftentimes these purported supernatural occurrences are not even brought before the Church to consider as legitimate because the process is too lengthy and demands abundant proof. While this is a prudent precaution for the Church to take, it also means Father Jose's story may never be formally approved by the Church.

Father Jose remains a loyal servant of the Church, always making Christ and His Kingdom the focus of his healing ministry. The priest doesn't allow the local media to interview him anymore because they have published stories in which it appears that Father Jose is the healer and not God.

"I am not the healer," the priest says emphatically, adding that he is merely the Lord's instrument. Father Jose was interviewed on EWTN, and he continues to cooperate with media who clearly convey this point to their audiences.

Father Jose does not use his name in reference to the ministry. Instead, he calls it a Eucharistic healing ministry so people stay focused on the true source of healing – Jesus.

"The Eucharist is the main part of our faith because it is Jesus. And the Eucharist and the priesthood are well connected. There is no priest if there is no Eucharist," he said.

This Christ-centered, sacramental approach is why miracles abound whenever Father Jose is praying nearby.

"If I may touch but His clothes, I shall be whole" (Mark 5:28)

Thousands of miracles have been attributed to God working through this priest. Father Jose values spiritual healings above all else. Having seen the eternal torments of hell, and the suffering in Purgatory, Father Jose is keenly aware of the spiritual dimension to our world and ardently tries to make people aware of it before it's too late. His sermons are unusually clear and unambiguous about the dangers of sin and the possibility of going to hell.

"I'm very concerned when people are living in mortal sin. It makes me very unhappy and sad, it even makes me sick, because I have seen souls in hell, lots of souls," he said. "The purpose of my story and my ministry is to help people avoid hell..."

The priest also takes time to marvel at the physical miracles God performs through him.

MIRACLES ABOUND

John Bryan Hobbs and his wife, Lily, will never forget the spiritual and physical miracles they received through the prayers of Father Jose.

When the couple married they practiced different Christian faiths. John was a good Baptist, and Lily, a devout Catholic. They had their theological differences but they loved each other, and they worshiped the same God. That was enough for them, until they started having children.

Then it began to matter more where they went to

church and what faith they would raise their children in. Lily asked Father Jose to pray for her husband's conversion so she could pass down the faith right alongside her husband.

Father Jose went to work praying for John, and it quickly began to show. John started coming to Mass regularly with Lily, and one day after Mass, he told her he wanted to join the Rite of Christian Initiation for Adults, a period of guided study and reflection on Church teachings for those wishing to enter the Catholic Church. But he also made something clear – he didn't want to convert, he just wanted to learn.

So Father Jose continued praying, and also started fasting for John. At the end of RCIA John told Lily, "I want to be Catholic now."

It took one year for John's conversion since Lily asked Father Jose for his prayers. Today, Father Jose is John's spiritual director and John and Lily have three young children – Philip, Anna Marie and Maria Elise.

QUIET, GENTLE SPIRIT

Lily also received two physical healings through the intercessory prayers of Father Jose. When she was six months pregnant with her second child, Anna Marie, Lily's doctor told her the baby had Down Syndrome, and she had the option to abort her. Lily was rattled by both the diagnosis and her doctor's quick suggestion that she get rid of her child.

She immediately went to Father Jose for prayer, and afterward she felt at peace. A month later she went back to the doctor where they did more testing, but this time there were no signs of the previously obvious diagnosis of Down Syndrome. A few months later Anna Marie was born perfectly healthy. She is now 5 years old, and her mother describes her as a "quiet, gentle spirit," who dreams of becoming a nun one day.

Lily's next miracle came when she was pregnant with her third child, Maria. Doctors told Lily she had an obstruction in her womb that was preventing the baby from receiving enough food and oxygen to survive. This would likely result in a permanent mental handicap. Doctors predicted the baby would live only six months. Lily immediately went to Father Jose for prayer and felt at peace again.

Maria was born three weeks premature, but otherwise healthy. The doctors were amazed. Lily cuddled her newborn baby and thanked God for His many blessings.

TOTAL PEACE

One morning in 2006 Priscilla Wenner woke up and looked in the mirror – she had a lump on her neck. "That's odd," she thought.

The next morning, another lump appeared on her neck. This time, she went to her primary care doctor who said it was probably swollen lymph nodes, attributable to an earlier sinus infection. She gave Priscilla new antibiotics to treat it.

But a few weeks later Priscilla was back in the doctor's office. The lumps were still there, and her doctor referred her to an Ear Nose and Throat doctor. Unfortunately, her insurance policy was changing so she saw a different specialist instead.

He told her she had an infection, and changed her antibiotic one more time. Priscilla came in for a check up every other week for the next six weeks without any signs of improvement. In fact, her lumps were getting much worse. They were on her neck and face now, and she couldn't sleep comfortably.

Finally, Priscilla grew weary and called her primary care doctor back for advice, and she suggested she go to an Otolaryngologist, or an Ear Nose and Throat doctor

In ten seconds, the new doctor had diagnosed Priscilla.

"These are dead cells," he said. "And do you know what causes dead cells?"

"No," Priscilla replied.

"Cancer," he said, gravely. He ordered a biopsy, and the results confirmed that it was lymphoma.

Priscilla then went to an oncologist, a doctor specializing in cancer, who ordered a biopsy of her bone marrow that confirmed she had stage four cancer.

When the results came back, Priscilla's family was in tears – she would need to begin chemotherapy immediately. Priscilla, who seemed to be in very good health and experienced no symptoms besides the lumps, was surprised by the diagnosis.

She immediately went to Father Jose for prayers. Priscilla had been attending his monthly healing Masses for a year, and although she wasn't sick, she went because the Masses were spiritually uplifting. Priscilla, a seamstress, would occasionally fix a zipper or hem a pair of pants for the priest free of charge as a way of saying thank you for his ministry. Over time they became good friends.

When she told Father Jose she had stage 4 cancer, he

said, "Don't worry about it. You are going to be ok. I have been praying for you, and asking the Blessed Mother for her prayers, and we know that you are going to be ok. You are going to experience some pain, and a lot of sickness, but that's normal. Just accept it and offer it up," he said. Then he prayed over her adding, "You won't feel any anxiety or fear during this suffering."

After their conversation, Priscilla's worry vanished, and she left everything up to God.

She told Father Jose, "You told me the cancer is going to be gone, and I know it's going to be gone."

While Priscilla was going through cancer treatments her doctor was amazed – her pulse and blood pressure stayed normal and she remained in good spirits. When a nurse asked her how the treatments were going, Priscilla responded saying she was tired and nauseous, but she knew that was normal. Then she asked Priscilla what her tumor marker was, and she was surprised when Priscilla said she didn't know. A tumor marker is a substance in the body that help's determine a patient's response to treatment, and if they are improving.

"Why don't you know?" she asked, curious.

"Because a special priest told me I was going to be ok, and I believe him, so I don't need to know what my tumor marker is," Priscilla replied. The nurse walked out of the room shaking her head in disbelief.

During chemotherapy Priscilla lost 40 pounds and suffered considerably, but she never lost her positive attitude. After six months of treatment, the doctor ordered Priscilla to take another biopsy because he couldn't feel any more cancerous lymph nodes.

Priscilla knew she was finally cured, and the test results confirmed her belief – the cancer was gone. Priscilla has been cancer free for six years.

"Every time I thank Father Jose he says, 'Don't thank me, thank the Blessed Mother and God,'" Priscilla said.

But Father Jose's help and prayers didn't end after her cancer left, Priscilla said. Father Jose called her to ask if she would bring her 43-year-old daughter, Bonnie, who had Down Syndrome, to morning Mass the following Tuesday.

"Of course, father," she said. But he called her again, later in the week, just to make sure she was coming.

"Yes, father, you know that I enjoy coming to morning Mass with you," Priscilla responded, slightly confused by his persistence.

Before morning Mass that Tuesday, Father Jose spent 15 seconds praying over Priscilla and about five minutes praying over Bonnie.

"That was unusual of him to pray over her for so long," she thought.

After Mass, Priscilla and her daughter met up with some friends at a nearby park. It was a beautiful, balmy day in Florida, and they spent more than an hour outside, talking. As Priscilla was getting up to go, Bonnie made a gagging noise and passed out.

She wasn't breathing, but her heart was still beating, so Priscilla rushed her to the hospital where she was taken directly into surgery. But the doctors couldn't bring her back to life. An aneurism had burst inside her, and she died almost instantly.

When Father Jose arrived to the hospital Priscilla asked him, "Did you know Bonnie was going to die today?" Father

Jose didn't respond, and he walked over to Bonnie to give her a blessing.

Later he told Priscilla, "I knew when she died. I saw her go up to heaven."

Father Jose, seven other priests and three deacons celebrated Bonnie's packed funeral Mass. Bonnie was loved by the community and especially the priests, because she would make them laugh with her candidness. "Oh, go take a hike!" she would say to her pastor.

Priscilla looks back on the event, and remembers how calm and peaceful she felt at her daughter's passing. She knows this peace came from God through the prayers of Father Jose.

LABOR OF LOVE

Father Jose looks back on his motorcycle accident and understands why it happened on the Feast of Jesus' Divine Mercy. It was a heavenly reminder to Father Jose and everyone who comes to him for prayers, that the healing love and mercy they experience in his ministry is not from him, but from God alone.

Father Jose is scrupulous about never taking credit for God's work, even though his ministry schedule is grueling. He receives a minimum of 100 emails a day and 60 phone calls a day. Often, he stays up until the early hours of the morning responding to emails of people asking for healing prayers, only to rise at 5 am and begin the day again. But Father Jose has not forgotten Mary's promise – made in heaven – to help him in his ministry, and he often asks her to pray for his strength.

Father Jose summarizes his ministry saying it's about "God's mercy coming through me, through my life, and through my actions."

For more information on Father Jose and his healing ministry please go to www.frmaniyangathealingministry.com.

Father Jose Maniyangat blesses a man following Mass at St. Catherine of Sienna Parish in Orange Park Fl. where he currently celebrates a monthly healing Mass.
(Photo Courtesy of Father Jose Maniyangat)

*John Bryan Hobbs, his wife Lily and their three children – Anna
Marie, Philip and Marie (left to right) – smile for a recent Easter
photo at their church, St. Catherine of Sienna Parish in Orange
Park Fl. Father Jose prayed over Lily while she was pregnant
with Anna Marie and Maria. Each time she received a miracle.
(Photo Courtesy of Lily Hobbs)*

4 | STELLA DAVIS

"I can do all things through Christ who strengthens me."
Philippians 4:13

Someone is rustling through the liquor cabinet as Mass is being celebrated at Stella Davis' house. A seminarian in need of deliverance has found a brief refuge in a bottle of brandy during Holy Communion. Stella confronts him, and splashes the sink with the remaining liquor. Then come the unearthly, foreign languages, ones you don't know and can't learn by going to school – Stella and her group of believers are speaking in tongues and laying their hands on the seminarian in prayer. Occasionally someone shouts over the small but mighty choir of older ladies unceasingly reciting the Chaplet of Divine Mercy.

Groans and more shouts ensue – but this time they are different, darker, as the seminarian is being delivered. The hum of the women praying the Chaplet grows stronger, it continues like this for hours, and the sounds almost become commonplace. And then it's over, for now. The seminarian leaves, and the small army of praying women become a gaggle of chattering, friendly ladies who share a meal together.

CONSTANT PRAYER, CONSTANT

Stella and her group meet every Monday morning in her Vienna Virginia home to drive out demons and pray over people who come to them seeking help that they can find no where else.

Stella readily admits that not every Monday morning meeting is quite that eventful, but miracles do have a tendency to crop up whenever she is nearby. Through her, God has healed the sick, brought nonbelievers to the faith, and delivered those tormented by demons.

After doing God's work in the healing ministry for more than 38 years the supernatural has become natural to Stella. She has little, if any, fear of the demonic.

Psalm 23, "The Lord is my Shepard," and Psalm 91, "He is my defender," are Scripture passages Stella lives by.

But Stella doesn't seem like the demon-fighting, miracle-working type. Instead, she gives the distinct first impression of being a sweet old lady with many well-loved grandchildren.

Only the active observer would notice the large Benedictine Crucifix that hangs low around her neck. It is used for casting out demons and for protection against them. This is the crucifix worn by everyone on Stella's prayer team.

She relies on her team for constant, zealous prayer while God works miracles through her.

Without prayer Stella says her ministry would fail.

Her husband of 56 years, John Davis, converted their porch into a fully finished chapel that Stella prays in daily.

Inside the chapel rests an abundance of religious artwork. An image of Our Lady of Guadalupe graces the front of the altar. Mass has been celebrated in this chapel many times, including once by a bishop.

But even among the many religious images Stella feels the keen absence of Jesus in the Blessed Sacrament in her own chapel. She goes to church and spends four to five hours in prayer in front of the Eucharist before a healing service or a speaking engagement. Here, in front of Jesus, the Holy Spirit blesses and equips her with strength and wisdom.

In the car, or in between daily activities, Stella also fits in countless Rosaries and Chaplets of Divine Mercy. She regularly meditates on God's Word, and references the Bible in everyday conversation. Prayer is foundational if you want to follow Jesus, she says.

Every day and late at night she fields phone calls from people asking for healing prayer. Her healing ministry has taken her around the world, where hundreds of people have come to receive God's healing touch through Stella.

Prompted by two Maryknoll sisters who studied with her at the University of Steubenville, Stella traveled to Japan where she met a missionary priest struggling to win converts.

For 25 years he taught English to Japanese men while also introducing them to Christianity. But the men were unfamiliar with Western religions and reluctant to listen to stories of Jesus.

When Stella arrived – a petite, Catholic woman from the West – the chance of these men placing their confidence in her and converting appeared slim.

She became acutely aware of her inability to reach these men when she prayed to God for guidance and didn't receive any. It wasn't until she arrived to the church hall filled with about 35 Japanese men that God gave her one word to dwell on, "Challenge."

The rest of God's message came to her just as the priest introduced her to the crowd – "Challenge them to your faith."

"OK, that's easy," she said to herself, and standing before the crowd of unbelieving men she told them the story of Jesus – from His birth to His death and resurrection. She spoke as if she was reading from a children's book – slowly, plainly, and with great love.

But God knew the men needed more than the story of His love – they needed proof. Trusting in God completely, Stella read a passage from Scripture about Jesus' healing power, and asked if anyone would like to see His power for themselves.

Curiosity filled the room and Stella asked for someone in pain to volunteer to be prayed over. A man who suffered from chronic and severe back pain came forward.

Involved in a traumatic accident, he had undergone several back surgeries without success. He was forced to live and work with agonizing pain so he could support his family.

Assured of God's love for these men, Stella began to pray, placing her hand on the injured man's forehead and back.

There, in front of everyone, he began to weep. To his

amazement he could now bend over. The pain was gone.

That night two more suffering men asked for Stella to pray over them and they were healed – one couldn't stop laughing with joy and the other gave Stella a warm embrace. The men could no longer conceal their emotions as their stoic culture prescribed – Jesus had healed them.

Stella then asked, "Would you like to receive this Jesus into your hearts who I know has given me that power?"

Stella was happy to discover that not just the three men who were healed wanted to know Jesus, but all 35 men did.

God had finally answered the faithful missionary priest's prayers. He told Stella before she left, "Stella, my dear child, I've been trying to do this for 25 years and God has done it through you in 15 minutes!"

No Señora

Thousands of miles away and several years later, Stella traveled to Lima, Peru on another mission trip. She was invited by a Peruvian judge and his wife to minister to the people of the city and people in remote, impoverished villages.

They set up speaking engagements for Stella throughout the region, and one outdoor conference drew hundreds of people who gathered in the early morning hours just to secure a spot.

But one of the most powerful experiences Stella had in Peru wasn't on the itinerary. This divine appointment took place as Stella toured the home of her favorite saint, Martin de Porres.

At age 13, Stella read a book about the mystical saint

who is known for his love of the poor and the extraordinary gifts he received from God. St. Martin would have ecstasies that lifted him into the air, light flooded the room when he prayed, and miracles happened often around him. The story of his life made a deep impression on Stella who prayed she would follow in the great saint's footsteps.

St. Martin's home now serves as a haven for the less fortunate. The elderly and the poor eat at a soup kitchen there, and St. Martin's bedroom was converted into a chapel. On her tour of the home Stella stopped in the chapel to pray, but the urgent shouting of her assistant soon interrupted her.

Stella hurried out of the chapel and onto the patio where she saw two women fighting – one of them violently wielded a machete. They were working in the kitchen when the fight began and it had spilled out onto the patio where everyone from the soup kitchen was eating.

It was God's grace coupled with Stella's 'yes' to God's call that led her directly into the fray.

As Stella ran toward the quarrel she could hear the people gathered on the patio calling out for her to stop, shouting, "No Señora, No Señora!"

When she reached the women she raised her hand up and commanded Satan to drop the machete. The weapon immediately fell to the ground, as did the woman who brandished it. She lay there, resting in the Spirit, while Stella ministered to the other woman, who said her attacker mistakenly thought she was having an affair with her husband.

Soon afterward the director of operations at the house asked what should be done with the woman who was still lying on the ground.

Stella instructed the director not to move her, she placed a rosary around her neck and prayed over her. The woman returned to full consciousness and was no longer violent. But Stella's work there wasn't finished – everyone who saw the event unfold knew God was working through her, and they asked her for healing prayers.

Stella thinks fondly of God's providence in this event. There she was – in the home of the mystical saint she cherishes – and Stella led a healing service for the poor while the woman and her fallen machete lay close-by.

God is good, Stella says. And St. Martin surely had this on the itinerary all along.

A FAMILY AFFAIR

The saint – who experienced attacks from the devil during his lifetime – was probably also watching over Stella when the devil pushed her down a winding iron staircase.

The attack occurred during a trip she took to Chicago at the request of her close friend, George. His cousin was preparing for an operation to remove breast cancer, and George told them about Stella's healing charism.

"The Lord will heal you if she prays for you," he declared boldly.

And while his relatives were only nominally Catholic they found the confidence in his statement reassuring, and they agreed for Stella to come and pray.

But George had doubts as they drove.

"Maybe we should have brought more people to pray with us," he said to Stella, who reassured him that God was in control.

George fasted and prayed all the way to his cousin's house where a crowd of almost 30 people met them. Many were fallen away Catholics or unbelievers who ached for the chance to be healed of their bodily ills with out any idea that what they really needed was spiritual healing.

They all crowded into the basement for the healing service that lasted five hours. Many people received spiritual healing that night. George's cousin was healed of her breast cancer.

During the following night's healing service more healings occurred. A father and his 21-year-old son forgave each other after a long period of estrangement. George's nephew received a physical healing. He had hurt his back in a football game that day, and the pain was so intense he could barely move. After Stella prayed over him she asked the young man to bend down, and to his disbelief, the pain was gone.

George's brother, skeptical, kept asking his nephew, "Are you sure you don't hurt anymore?"

The answer remained "No."

LIFE AFTER DEATH

George's relatives were slowly becoming acquainted with the supernatural because God was preparing them for what was to come.

It was 11 o'clock at night – just as Stella had finished ministering to George's relatives and she was going upstairs to pick up her briefcase and jacket – that she felt a strong push and tumbled down 16 stairs, hitting her back and neck along the way. Her hand caught on the iron railing and three fingers bent completely backward. By the time she hit the bottom of the stairs Stella had died. It was an attack from the enemy.

She remembers lying in a heap on the floor when her spiritual body swept upward out of her flesh. The higher she would go, the brighter things became. She could see her husband and children back home, but her love for them was eclipsed by the indescribable love she was receiving.

She continued to climb upward until a voice stopped her heavenly trajectory – "You must go back," Jesus said.

But Stella refused – she wanted only to bask in that infinite love.

"Your work is not finished," Jesus said, and even before His words were spoken Stella plummeted back down toward her physical body, and her spirit returned to her flesh. She could hear George and his wife, Mary, crying.

"What am I going to tell her husband? That I killed her?" George cried.

The owner of the house was shouting, "Call the rescue squad! I'm not going to have her die in my house!"

Then George frantically urged everyone to start praying.

Stella found herself in crippling pain. Her body was limp, and when George picked her up to place her on the couch she began to shake uncontrollably – she was in shock.

That's when George said, "Okay, let's call the ambulance," and as he uttered those words Stella felt as if she had been plugged into an electrical socket. Her shaking grew even more violent, but she could no longer feel the pain.

She asked George to help her up, but she fell down and

had to be placed in a chair. She looked down and saw a bone sticking out of her leg.

Stella directed George to get the holy oil, anoint her leg and push the bone in.

George, acting on nerves and faith, did as he was asked. When the bone slipped back into Stella's flesh it felt like suction, he later recalled.

While George anointed Stella's ailing body parts, his family members looked on with shocked awe. Stella had recovered. Her last request was that George use the holy oil to straighten her fingers.

As he finished, Stella asked for her jacket and briefcase – she was ready to leave. George's cousin pleaded with her to at least get an x-ray but she declined. The injuries were gone, but Stella still continues to ponder the cherished memory of that next-life encounter with Our Lord.

GOD'S PEOPLE

While Stella's mystical spiritual life is at times incomprehensible, it is perhaps her sincere love of the poor and forgotten that make her experiences more tangible.

Just ask Jim. Before he met Stella, loneliness consumed him. The small elderly man had taken to drinking at a young age after an abnormal hump on his back stunted his growth and left him standing at just 5 feet tall. At age 16 he left home and began working odd jobs to earn just enough money to buy food and wine. He never raised a family of his own, and he felt purposeless.

At the time he met Stella, he lived friendless and alone in a rundown senior citizen welfare complex. Twice a week

Jim came into the social work office where Stella volunteered to ask if they needed any help, and to pass the time. While others in the office would grow weary of Jim, Stella spent her free moments listening to his stories over a shared pot of coffee. He invited her to his apartment, but for no particular reason, she was never able to make it there.

It wasn't until many years later when she was driving by his place that the Holy Spirit inspired Stella to visit Jim.

She asked him why God had sent her there, and Jim smiled, because he knew that his prayers had been answered. Jim's unrelenting loneliness led him to pass the time with booze and cigarettes, and in his anguish he asked God to lift him out of this dark hole that he couldn't escape from alone.

Stella was an answer to that prayer. The first thing she did was clean Jim's apartment, and buy new curtains for the windows. She would spend hours talking with Jim and – like he was her own father – Stella often invited him to her house for dinner and the holidays. He became a fixture in their home – attending Stella's son's football games, picking apples with her children, and staying with them for days at a time. All the while Stella helped Jim give up his addictions, and grow closer to Christ. He had learned what it meant to be loved, and so he finally learned to love himself in return.

When Jim died Stella and her husband drove hundreds of miles in heavy snow to bury him where he was raised in West Virginia.

Stella providentially arrived to see Jim's sisters discussing with their pastor what to say about him at the funeral, and they were clearly discouraged. His sisters had not seen Jim since he left home at 16. They only knew the old Jim, not the new Jim who loved the Lord, and felt peace in his heart.

When Stella read them a letter from Jim's pastor about his remarkable conversion, tears streamed down their faces. Stella remembers one of her last looks at Jim – lying in his casket wearing a blue suit and the faintest trace of a smile etched across his face.

Stella could hear him saying "I am very happy," and she replied, "Jimmy boy, I'll see you later."

Stella has had many friends like Jim, and she has also formed organizations that serve people in need on a larger scale.

In 1975, God placed in Stella's heart an idea for a women's group dedicated to winning souls for Jesus, and serving others. The group – made up of both Protestant and Catholic women – began sharing the love of Christ with elderly people who lived just outside Washington, D.C. in a poor area with a high crime rate. Their living conditions were depressing and often unhealthy. Stella discovered that many of them weren't eating enough, and as a result they couldn't focus on the message of God's love.

Stella remedied this problem by asking her group to cook a meal for them each week.

"We loved them, fed them, and sang and prayed with them," Stella remembers.

For one elderly blind man, he could see and smell when the women arrived each Thursday. They would stroll with him down the street – describing everything on their path and bringing flowers to his nose to smell.

There is also a spot in Stella's heart carved out for children with disabilities. While living on an Army base with her husband she learned of a program for exceptional children in the Protestant church there. She asked the church's pastor if she could combine both Protestant and Catholic children and teach the children about Jesus herself.

He agreed, and every Sunday children on wheel chairs, crutches and braces lined the streets to be picked up by the bus that took them to class with "Mrs. Davis." One 15-year-old-boy with Down Syndrome, Victor, died the second year Stella taught the class. After three heart attacks Victor joined the Lord in heaven.

His mother told Stella that a few days before he died Victor said he was in a hurry to be with Jesus because, "Mrs. Davis said it is beautiful living and walking with Jesus."

Through Stella, many have felt the loving arms of Jesus wrapped around them.

In 1991, the Holy Spirit filled Stella's heart and helped her write these prophetic words about the chapel in her home and the continuation of her ministry:

"My beloved children let it be made known to you that I have chosen this sanctuary to reveal My presence, to reveal My healing power. Let it be a house of prayer ... Go forth from this place and know that My love, My joy, and My peace and My healing have touched you this day."

The truth of this message is still fully alive in Stella and her ministry today.

For more information on Stella and her healing ministry please go to www.cwiaholyspirit.org.

Stella (center) poses with Msgr. John Brady (left) and Auxiliary Bishop Victor Tamayo Bentancourt, bishop of Barranquilla Colombia, during Stella's 2012 Women's Conference in Alexandria, Va. Stella's non-profit organization, Christian Women In Action, is helping build a church in a poor village in Barranquilla. (Photo Courtesy of Stella Davis)

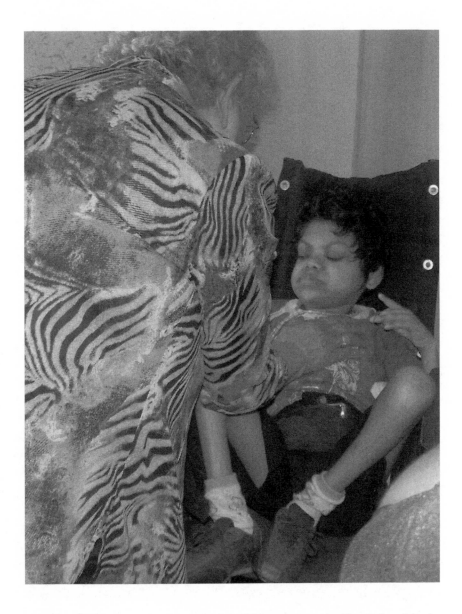

Stella prays for a hospitalized child in Barranquilla Colombia in this 2011 photo. (Photo Courtesy of Stella Davis)

5 | FATHER RICHARD MCALEAR

"And truly Jesus did many other signs in the presence of His disciples, which are not written in this book; but these are written that you may believe that Jesus is the Christ, the Son of God, and that believing you may have life in His name." John 20:30-31

The first time Kim Combs and her sister met Father Richard McAlear or "Father Mac" they couldn't stop talking about his unforgettable blue eyes. "Crystal clear and beautiful," she said. "He radiated God's love."

A year later, when she saw him again, Kim did a double take – Father Mac's eyes were an ordinary brown color. When she told Father Mac, an Oblate of Mary Immaculate, he didn't seem surprised. He had heard it all before. The brown eyed priest has been told many times that his eyes turn a clear blue during the healing service.

Donna Rittereiser, who worked for Father McAlear and coordinated all of his healing services while at Ave Maria University in Naples, Florida, also had a mystical experience while being prayed over during one of the healing services. Donna does not remember a defining moment when the priest's eyes changed from brown to blue, but as Father McAlear prayed over her she felt like she was looking into the eyes of Jesus, and she described his eyes as "The bluest blue I've ever seen." Donna finds it challenging to fully explain this experience to others, but realizes that because it was a personal and supernatural gift from God it may never be completely understood.

She was even more surprised to discover that her husband, Tom, had the same experience that evening. "We were both overwhelmed and it took some time to absorb this special experience," Donna said. "We both felt God's intense love and peace flow through Father McAlear as he prayed over us."

During all of Fr. McAlear's healing services, the Blessed Sacrament remains exposed on the altar. Reflecting on this, Donna said, "The true gift which Jesus gives us is His true presence in the Blessed Sacrament. Jesus revealing Himself, truly present, at Mass, in the Blessed Sacrament, at the healing service."

"With a lot of prayer and discernment about this experience, we felt that God allowed us to have this mystical encounter with Him, this gift, for a reason. And as we know, with receiving this gift, so much more is expected," Donna said. "We now had to take this gift and translate it into our lives — to pray more, to give witness, to love more and be examples for others."

During a healing Mass Father Mac often looks at each person while he prays over them. Many who have come to him with heavy burdens, have felt their loads completely lifted. This is Father Mac's unique charism – to heal heavy hearts and broken souls. One of his favorite Bible passages is, "Come to me all you who are labored and burdened and I will give you rest," (Matthew 11:28). This characterizes his ministry well.

When Kim Combs' son-in-law died in a fatal car crash leaving her daughter with three young children to raise, Kim felt depressed thinking about how they would make it without him. A lingering sadness filled her soul.

But the first day Father Mac prayed over her she felt God's peace and love envelop her. Her worries faded and her joy resumed. Father Mac's blue eyes were an outward sign that God's love was truly coming through this humble priest to heal her heart.

Her 8-year-old grandson who suffered the loss of his father experienced that same healing love. He asked Kim why some people fell down during the healing service, and although she tried to explain, the best answer came later, when the priest prayed over the boy and he immediately fell down.

Later he told Kim, "Grandma, I don't know what happened, but when I looked at that man, I saw the face of Jesus and I couldn't stand up."

The young and old alike feel this ethereal love in the priest's presence. Many elderly people who the priest prays over say they have never had someone look at them so lovingly before.

Eighty-one year old Delores Kiernan felt that love and peace both times she attended Father Mac's healing Masses.

Before meeting Father Mac, Delores had a terrifying experience. The defibrillator she needed for her weak heart malfunctioned and shocked her 41 times before she could get to the hospital where they could turn it off.

Each time the defibrillator shocked her it threw her to the ground and she saw a flash of light – she thought she was going to die.

Delores was further petrified when the doctor told her she would need to get a new one. Resistant, she asked him if he would recommend this for his own mother, and he reluctantly said yes.

So she followed his instructions, but remained anxious, forever awaiting the next jolt to ricochet through her body. She couldn't turn on a light without flashbacks, and she often daydreamed of living out in the woods and leaving electricity behind.

It was around this time that she saw an announcement for Father Mac's healing Mass at her parish and she decided to go.

With little knowledge of what to expect, Delores approached Father Mac for prayers following the Mass. As soon as he began praying, she fell to the ground.

When she woke she no longer felt anxious, but totally at peace.

"I had no control over it, but I felt like I was on a glider going down," she said. "I wanted to stay in that church forever."

The second time she went to Father Mac's healing Mass, Delores made up her mind not to fall down. She thought she could stop it because she knew what it felt like. But Delores was no match for God who gently placed her back on the ground when Father Mac prayed over her.

Delores asked another priest why this happened, and he said that God was healing her. Delores agreed, and since Father Mac's prayers she has felt tremendous peace and has had no heart problems.

Father Mac frequently reminds people who come to his healing Masses that everyone has hurts in their lives and they need to be healed of those hurts. He accomplishes this by preaching about Jesus' divine love, encouraging forgiveness and proclaiming Jesus' real presence in the Blessed Sacrament.

Following every Mass, Father Mac begins the healing service with the exposition of the Blessed Sacrament on the altar, because he believes the greatest healing comes through Jesus in the Eucharist.

He explains his focus on the Eucharist by illuminating the Incarnation: "The central mystery to all Christianity is the Incarnation. The work of salvation and the fruits of the Spirit flow from this one fundamental truth of the Word made flesh. Jesus is Emmanuel – God with us. The Eucharist is His continuing presence in our midst."

During Mass he encourages those receiving the Holy Eucharist to begin their healing journey by taking their needs and infirmities to the Lord as they receive the Eucharist.

"With the Holy Eucharist within us, and the Holy Eucharist exposed before us, we are embraced by the Merciful Heart of Jesus," he said.

Many liken the gentle-spirited priest to St. Padre Pio, a mystical Italian saint known for bearing the supernatural wounds of Christ on his hands and reading the hearts of penitents who flocked to him. The saint also had a healing charism, and a deep, unforgettable love of people.

It is this same magnetizing love of people that Father Mac is known for. When the priest prays for people he always feels their emotional pain, and sometimes he feels their physical pain too. This keen awareness of others needs deepens his compassion for those he serves.

Raised in Boston, Father Mac was the second of five boys born to an Italian mother and an Irish father. The parish was the center of their world, and they participated in Sunday Mass, first Friday devotions, May processions and attended the parish school. Here, in his parish home, Father Mac's vocation to the priesthood was fostered. He left for seminary directly after high school. He studied in Rome and was ordained to the priesthood in 1970 after receiving degrees in philosophy and theology.

But Father Mac had still not discovered his spiritual gift of healing. He considered himself a devotional Catholic who loved Jesus, but who had very little understanding of spiritual gifts.

It wasn't until two years after his ordination that Father Mac's healing charism was discovered. During a prayer meeting he was attending, people were trying to figure out what should be done about a woman who had come to the meeting in severe pain. Earlier that day, as she was painting her kitchen, she took doors off their hinges and laid them across the counters. When she returned to pick up a bucket of paint, the doors fell on top of her and injured her back. She came to the prayer meeting hoping the pain would dissipate, but instead it grew much worse. Every position and movement was excruciating. While some talked of taking her to the emergency room, one lady, a former Pentecostal and convert to Catholicism, asked Father Mac to pray over the injured woman.

"You want me to do what?" Father Mac asked, clearly unfamiliar with the expression 'pray over.'

Unsure of what was being asked of him, Father Mac reluctantly complied. He gave the woman a standard blessing and she was instantly healed of her back pain. She could now sit, move around, and bend over. She was no longer in pain. She was completely recovered. Onlookers were amazed.

Father McAlear left the prayer meeting slightly confused, pondering in his heart over what had just happened. He wondered why God had chosen him – a man who was so unacquainted with this aspect of his faith – to heal.

The next week at the prayer meeting the woman returned – still in perfect health. Father Mac was ambushed with requests for blessings that he couldn't say no to. Soon people started coming from farther away to be prayed over by the priest and inviting him to their parishes to pray for the sick. Slowly, Father Mac grew more comfortable with the gift God had so suddenly given him. Father has since devoted his life to his healing ministry. Today, he travels throughout the world taking God's message of healing love to people.

"All over the world – from the jungles of Papua New Guinea, to the deserts of Australia to the streets of New York – when people get sick they get the same desperation, the same fear," Father McAlear told the Scottish Catholic Observer during a mission in Scotland in 2011. Father Mac was surprised how many tough Scots opened up to him as he prayed over them. Some even cried as they felt their burdens being lifted.

Father Mac added that he doesn't think it's a coincidence that a large part of the Gospels are devoted to Jesus healing people. "I think that's how it happened," he said. "People came for the healing and stayed for the teaching."

When Father travels to places like Korea and China – where most people don't believe in Christ – the healing miracles touch the people far more deeply than they do in the West. The miracles always result in large numbers of converts.

"They see Him (Christ) alive and at work in the ministry," Father Mac said. "There is faith there. You say He is alive, and they believe He is alive when miracles happen."

In the United States, the pervasive secularism and cynicism can prevent people from opening up their hearts to God for healing.

"Sometimes it's harder to reach people because of it," Father Mac said. "We are technological, scientific – expect more, get less. Our faith is in science here ... We put layers between us and God."

Despite this hardness of heart, God still works miracles in the Unites States.

LORRAINE'S STORY

In March 2000, Lorraine Naimo, a 57-year-old retired fashion executive from Brooklyn, decided it was time to go to the doctor. Her symptoms were eerily similar to the ones she felt when doctors diagnosed her with the beginning stages of cervical cancer eight years earlier.

The doctor confirmed her fears. A sonogram and an MRI showed she had a cancerous mass, tumors and fibroids on her left ovary. The blood test level revealed cancer, too.

Lorrainne had undergone cone biopsy surgery to rid herself of the cancer years earlier. This time she was determined to fight it again. Her doctor said she would need surgery immediately and an additional MRI of the pelvic area and stomach to make sure the cancer hadn't spread. The test was scheduled for Friday morning.

On Thursday evening, Lorraine attended a healing Mass led by Father Mac in Brooklyn. Lorraine admits that she is not the kind of Catholic who normally attends healing Masses. But, upset and sick, she went with her sister Rose hoping for some help. The night was rainy and miserable – a perfect reflection of how she felt inside.

As Father Mac prayed – gently holding her face in his hands and looking into her eyes – she felt a strange, burning heat and intense tingling pass through her body. Lorraine braced for the worst. She thought she was having a heart attack.

It seemed tragically ironic – she had come for healing and received what she thought was a heart attack. She put her sister on alert in case she passed out. The sensation lasted for five more minutes after she returned to her seat. It ended as though it were trying to rip out of her body at her fingertips. Immediately she began to feel much better physically and mentally.

"If that wasn't a heart attack, what happened to me?" she thought. As soon as she got home she called her other sister, Marie, to tell her what happened.

Marie had prayed over Lorraine before a spinal surgery years earlier and asked her if she felt anything at that time, because sometimes – not always – that was how the Holy Spirit announced His healing presence.

She didn't feel anything then, but this time she did and she desperately wanted to know – did she receive a miracle? Marie had no answers.

Lorraine couldn't sleep that night. She tossed and turned thinking about her MRI early the next morning. At the hospital they said they would rush the report and have it to her doctor by Monday. When Lorraine walked into her doctor's office on Monday, her doctor and his partner were standing at the front receptionist desk, waiting for her.

They said, "We have been looking at your film and report and we are completely baffled."

She asked them why, and her doctor's only response was, "It's a miracle." The other doctor said, "Only God could do this." They couldn't find any cancer.

The doctors ordered Lorraine to take another MRI, but it came back exactly the same – the cancer was gone. Before Father Mac's prayers, three tests showed that Lorraine had cancer. After Father Mac's prayers three tests showed the cancer was gone. Lorraine received a miracle.

"I know what happened to me. God healed me. And no one is going to change my mind on that one," she said.

Since Lorraine's miracle, she has had several spine operations related to a spinal collapse, but no cancer has returned.

Lorraine hasn't seen Father McAlear lately because he hasn't come to her area, but her voice gets scratchy from tears when she thinks about his face, and the love that radiates from him.

"The minute I look into his eyes, I get an overwhelming feeling and I just cry," she said.

Lorraine, and many others, believe the love that radiates from Father Mac is not his own, but God's love coming through him. "All the hurt, the tiredness, and the anger just comes right out," she said. "Everything seems to vanish. It's like a weight has been lifted from you. The only word I can use to describe it is love. The feeling of nothing but love."

MY ANGEL BROTHER

The popular phrase "God works in mysterious ways," came to life for the MacMillan family as they found themselves praying for a miracle. Juliet MacMillan was 12 weeks pregnant when doctors told her an ultrasound showed her baby's bladder was enlarged and his urethra was completely blocked. He would need surgery for the condition between 16 and 22 weeks gestation or he wouldn't survive.

Juliet and her husband, Mark, were terrified. They had to wait four weeks while the baby remained in danger and extremely uncomfortable. The weekend following the diagnosis Juliet's family prayed for a miracle, and she attended Father McAlear's healing Mass. As he prayed over Juliet she remembers crying, and connecting eye-to-eye with the sincere and compassionate blue-eyed priest.

The next day, she went back to the hospital where they took another ultrasound. The doctor was stunned. The urethra had opened up and everything was completely normal. The doctor agreed with Juliet that it must have been a miracle because the baby had a complete blockage, not a partial blockage. While partial blockages can sometimes open up as pressure builds against the urethra, complete blockages must be corrected with surgery.

"There really is no explanation for it to happen medically," she remembers the doctor telling her.

But God's plan for the MacMillans didn't involve the perfect health of their baby. Connor Patrick, their second son, was born with serious health issues. He was diagnosed with Adams Oliver Syndrome, a rare genetic disorder that affects the baby's division of cells in the uterus. Connor's fingers hadn't fully developed, and he was missing toes. More seriously, he had seizures almost daily; and his brain couldn't process images or sound; he couldn't hold his head up because of low muscle tone. Connor relied on a feeding tube around-the-clock for food.

For the first several months Juliet and her husband took turns staying up all night to care for their sick child – feeding him and watching for seizures. Mark had to leave work for six months, and they applied for Medicare so a nurse could help with the demanding care. Connor was rushed to the emergency room 20 times and had seven hospitalizations in his short life. Even so, Jack Ryan, the MacMillans' first son, thought Connor was the perfect baby brother. Jack would always talk to Connor lovingly and playfully, never being told that Connor couldn't hear or see him.

Juliet remembers taking Connor to a different specialist for almost every part of his body, but she considers it a miracle that he never had any trouble at all with his bladder. God had completely healed that part of him, just as she had asked Him to.

During pregnancy, Juliet remembers begging God to "just let him be born. I will take care of whatever problems there may be, just let me hold him and take care of him."

God answered those prayers, granting her this request for the short time that was Connor's life. Soon after Connor turned one, Connor's muscle tone decreased so much that it became hard for him to breathe. To keep his airway open, he had to be held upright, with his head tilted just-so, whether he was asleep or awake.

"We just held him and loved him because that was all we could do," Juliet said.

Connor passed away from viral pneumonia on Dec. 4, 2009, the day before he would have turned 20 months old. The MacMillans were devastated by the loss of their son, but they never lost faith in God or His love for them.

"I was so happy to spend as much time as I did with him, and I felt lucky that he was able to be born, and that we were able to hold him. That is what I prayed for."

Three months after Connor's death, Juliet gave birth to another son on St. Patrick's Day and named him Patrick Ryan, the middle names of his two older brothers, to commemorate Connor's life and to "link the boys together."

Jack, who is now 7 years old, still talks about Connor all the time. He calls him his "angel brother" and asks him questions like, "Connor, which team do you think will win the football game tonight?" One time when Juliet mentioned something about Connor never having a chance to meet his baby brother, Patrick, Jack responded indignantly, "Yes, he did! They met in heaven before Patrick came to earth!"

God works in mysterious ways, Juliet concedes. But His ways are perfect, at once filled with incredible joys and incredible sorrows that are meant to perfect us and lead us to heaven in the end. Juliet and Mark remain unshakably certain that they will meet Connor there one day. He is their angel son.

TEARS

Father Mac understands the depth of suffering people experience, because God gifted him with the ability to feel their pain as he prays over them. Perhaps this constant reminder of suffering led Father Mac to write, "Tears" – a book intended to alleviate anxiety and suffering by connecting people with God through meaningful prayer.

"I never weep alone because You are there. Whatever Your plan for me and whatever Your will I know it is loving. You never abandon me. You are present in the darkness even when I feel alone," Father Mac writes.

Sometimes, it is suffering that stirs hardened hearts to search for God so He can change their lives.

A retired doctor who had put his faith in science and the modern world was suffering from multiple cancers when he reached out to God for help. He was skeptical of the healing Mass, but his family urged him to give it a try. When he came up to Father Mac for prayers, the unexpected happened – he was completely healed.

That same night he went to Confession for the first time in 45 years, and he changed his life. He started praying the rosary, participating in Mass and reveling in his newfound love of the Lord.

Many years later, the cancer returned and the doctor was dying. But this time, instead of being afraid, he was at peace. Father Mac remembers him saying, "Don't worry, I know where I am going now."

"That's a real healing. A healing on every level," Father Mac said. These are the kinds of healings that keep Father Mac motivated to continue his work, even if it is physically demanding. The priest suffers from debilitating arthritis of the spine but takes very little time off to recover from his illness.

Another significant part of Father Mac's ministry is teaching. When he received permission from the Oblates to enter full time into his healing ministry in 1975, he began leading more retreats and prayer services.

He encouraged priests to "touch the heart" of the people they serve.

He told the *Clarion Herald* that priests "need to have a ministry to receive the tears of another person. We need to touch pain, the heartaches, the brokenness and the sorrows. We need to show solidarity with them (the people we serve) – being there with them – so they are not alone."

BREATHING AGAIN

After walking up two or three steps Trudy Ballinger had to stop and catch her breath. This was a daily occurrence for Trudy, because her lungs remained in a continuous asthmatic state. In 1989, dangerous fumes came through the IRS ventilator system in Covington, Kentucky where she worked. A cleaning crew accidentally spilled a toxic chemical into the ventilator system, and eight hundred people went to the hospital, including Trudy.

Her lungs were irreversibly damaged, and doctors told Trudy – then in her thirties – to "get your affairs in order" because they weren't sure if she would survive long. She couldn't walk without sitting and resting often, and she couldn't breathe without a constant stream of prescriptions and steroids to keep her asthma at bay. Trudy took seven prednisones a day, oxygen half the day and wore a CPAP mask for air at night.

After years of enduring this suffering, a relative invited her to a healing Mass. Trudy went without any expectations, just her pain. She was immediately comforted when she sensed Father Mac emanating an immense, unearthly love.

"His eyes would change, and so would the expression on his face," she said.

After Father Mac prayed over her he looked at her and said, "The healing hasn't started yet. Just give it time."

Trudy was baffled. "What did he mean by that?" she thought.

But as soon as Trudy left the Mass she could feel her lungs burning – God was healing her just as Father Mac had promised. When she returned home her husband asked if she needed help, and to his surprise, she said no. Trudy felt exactly how she did before the fateful accident that damaged her lungs.

Two days later, she had a doctor appointment, and she left without any prescriptions.

Her doctor said, "I don't know what you are doing but keep it up. I've never seen you feeling like this. I've never sent you out of here without prednisone or writing all kinds of prescriptions for you. What are you doing?"

With excitement, Trudy replied, "I had someone pray for me!"

Trudy, 54, now walks a couple miles each day, and hasn't taken any medications since she was healed. She jokingly claims she can "out-walk" anybody.

She also brought her son, Adam, who was involved with drugs to see Father Mac. Since his prayers Adam has stopped the drugs, and gone back to school and work. Trudy says she owes a lot to Father Mac for giving up his life to do God's work.

"I just felt so honored to be there at the healing Mass. God changed my life," she said.

Connor Patrick MacMillan sits on his older brother, Jack's, lap.
Jack spoke to Connor lovingly and playfully, never being told
that Connor couldn't hear or see him because of his illness.
Connor passed away when he was 19 months old.
(Photo Courtesy of Juliet MacMillan)

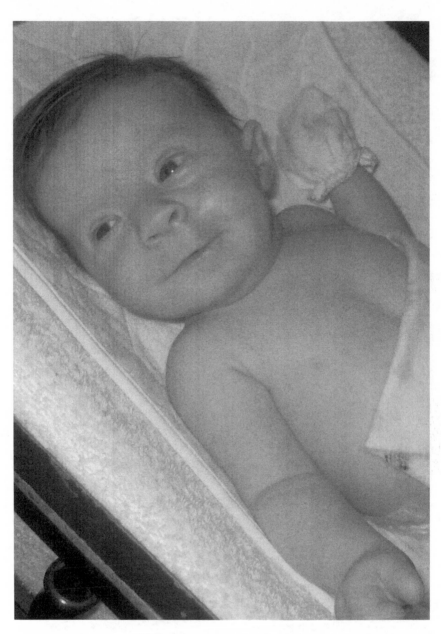

Connor Patrick MacMillan, who received a miracle while in utero, passed away when he was 19 months old from complications caused by Adam's Oliver syndrome. (Photo Courtesy of Juliet MacMillan)

Father Richard McAlear prays with several hundred women at a
retreat house in South Korea in 2010.
(Photo Courtesy of Father Richard McAlear)

Father Richard McAlear prays with survivors of the Rwandan genocide in this 2011 photo. The priest led a day of teaching and prayer to heal the scars of genocide for about one thousand survivors, mostly Tutsis, the ethnic group most targeted during the slaughter. (Photo Courtesy of Father Richard McAlear)

6 | FATHER DAN LEARY

"As the Father has loved me, so I have loved you.
Now remain in my love." John 15:9

The image of Father Dan Leary – walking across the hospital parking lot wearing his long black cassock – will never leave Angela Cunningham's mind.

Just one glance and he gave off the "I'm a traditional priest," vibe to Angela, an unbeliever.

She felt the urge to slip away, behind the cars and into the hospital where she needed to go. Experiencing pre-term labor six weeks before her due date, Angela was worried. But Father Dan was her brother's friend, and instead of running away she asked, "What are you doing here?"

Father Dan was visiting another patient in the hospital, but he was now focused on Angela.

Father Dan barely knew who she was so she wondered, "Why does he even care?"

But she couldn't refuse the blessing he gave her in the parking lot, and then she went inside. The doctors were not able to delay labor any longer, and Angela gave birth to her second child, Shannon.

EVERY 30 MINUTES

The new baby was the delight of her parents' hearts. But the joy of welcoming Shannon into the world was replaced with fear when doctors told them about her failing heart.

Shannon was transferred to Children's Hospital in Washington, DC where they discovered she had a multitude of heart problems. She was taken to the cardiac intensive care unit where she was hooked up to life support. The doctors told her distraught parents to prepare for her passing.

Every half an hour Shannon developed a new set of problems. Even after bleeding on the brain and a stroke, the tiny baby still clung to life.

Ironically, before Angela found out she was pregnant with Shannon – a pregnancy she had not planned – she and Jeffery were seriously considering divorce. They stayed married because of the baby, who could pass away at any moment and further shatter their already fragile relationship.

THREE HEARTS TO HEAL

It was Holy Week, the busiest week of the year for a pastor, but Father Dan had kept in touch with Angela after they met in the parking lot, and he decided to come pray over the baby. He drove more than an hour to Children's Hospital late at night. Angela was taken aback when he walked into the room.

"It was midnight and he took a piece of bread out of a bag and began to pray over her heart," she remembers. The piece of bread was the Eucharist, and as soon as Father Dan did this Angela's near-lifeless baby moved.

"It was like a spasm," she said. Angela didn't believe in God, but God pushed a small piece of Himself into her heart at that moment.

During the next three nights, Father Dan came back to pray over the baby, and on the third night – as he again held the Eucharist over Shannon's heart in prayer – she started breathing on her own over the life support machines.

Angela remembers looking at her daughter, who seemed illuminated, and letting the idea of God ruminate in her heart.

"It was like seeing Christ lying in that bed," she said. "It brought a peace to my heart that I had never felt before."

The next day, Shannon had improved – something doctors thought was impossible.

"So this heart that was a complete mess – that they didn't think they could surgically repair – started to heal itself. She started to breath on her own, the coarctation of the aorta and the regurgitation of the mitral valve repaired itself and she started turning around," Angela said.

Doctors no longer told Angela and Jeff to prepare for her impending death.

Jeff asked one doctor – a cardiologist for almost 50 years – why his daughter was suddenly getting better. "Was it the medication she was on? What happened?"

"No. If it was the medication I would tell you, but this was a miracle and your daughter was healed," he remembers the doctor saying.

The heavy medication also destroyed a nerve to Shannon's ear causing her to go deaf, but Father Dan prayed over her again, and she recovered her hearing.

"They said it was irreparable and now she can hear," Angela said.

Shannon, now 6 years old, still has a moderately severe heart condition, but her mother describes her as a happy and energetic child with an awareness of the spiritual world around her.

"She will offhandedly make comments like 'Yeah, when I was in the hospital I met Jesus,'" Angela said.

The story doesn't seem too farfetched for Angela, who also met Christ through her daughter's suffering in an interior way.

THE JOURNEY HOME

After these miracles, Angela decided to join the Rite of Christian Initiation for Adults, and become a confirmed Catholic. Jeff, already Catholic, renewed and deepened his faith alongside his wife.

Shannon and Father Dan still have a special connection. As Shannon grew older, she would doze off in Father Dan's arms as he prayed. Angela marveled at this because her daughter was such a fickle sleeper.

"Father Dan is very prayerful. Whenever he would pray the rosary with her she would rest in the spirit," Angela said.

Angela and Jeffery now have four children and they live a very active faith-life.

"The healing of Shannon is just one of the incredible gifts God gave us," Angela said. "Jesus in the Eucharist is what kept her alive, there is no doubt. Father Dan is just a beautiful vessel. He didn't have to come to the hospital. I wasn't even Catholic."

"I firmly believe that if Father Dan had not come and prayed with Shannon, and brought the Eucharist, she would not be alive today," Angela said.

Now when she thinks back on that first moment in the parking lot trying to escape Father Dan's blessing, she smiles. Father Dan acted as God's hands by reaching out to her, and calling her home.

A PARISH PRIEST

Father Dan Leary, 44, doesn't seem a day older than on his ordination day. The fun-loving pastor and chaplain to the Washington Redskins provides enough zeal to motivate even the most lackluster faithful. Many say his accessible, down-to-earth personality is what opened them up to deepening their relationship with Christ.

The priest – who loves a good joke and makes conversation easily – first draws people to God by expressing a genuine interest in becoming a friend. It's at this point that many people start to recognize Father Dan's deep reverence for the Catholic faith, and allow it to change their hearts.

Some people compare aspects of Father Dan's ministry to the ministry of St. John Vianney – drawing people back to the Church, lengthening the lines for Confession and generating a true love of Jesus in the Blessed Sacrament.

Laura Warlitner, a former secretary at Jesus the Divine Word Parish in Huntingtown, Md. who worked with Father Dan when he was pastor there, views Father Dan as an unassuming priest, who fully cooperates with God's grace in bringing souls to Jesus.

He is a "humble man who takes advantage of every opportunity to bring lost or wounded souls to Christ without expecting anything in return," she said.

She added that Father Dan thinks of himself as nothing special, but when he acts In Persona Christi, or In the Person of Christ, he becomes God's hands and feet in a very real way here on earth.

"He is well aware that his gift of healing belongs to God, and that it can be taken back at any time," she said.

HOLY MOTHER

While Father Dan often stresses that every priest is a healing priest, he also recognizes that God didn't fully reveal his own healing charism until after a trip to Mexico to learn Spanish and visit the Shrine of Our Lady of Guadalupe.

Father Dan, ordained seven years earlier, stayed at a convent three blocks away from the Shrine and he walked there every day to pray.

"During that time is when the grace came," he said. "Mary put her hands on my priesthood and began to lead me as she wanted me to be led."

When Father Dan returned home, he led a women's retreat, and the women began resting in the Spirit and sharing the beautiful healings they received.

"My natural reaction was 'oh this is fake' or 'this is overreaction,' but as I began to see the gift develop I thought to myself, 'It's impossible for this to be fake because it's too real,'" Father Dan said.

The key to using this gift, Father says, is to stay close to God in prayer while carefully listening to the promptings of the Holy Spirit. Aileen Vasquez remembers him saying, "I am afraid not to pray, because if I don't pray, everything I do is not going to work. It is useless."

Father Dan's healing ministry is strongly rooted in the Mass and the true presence of Christ in the Eucharist. With joy, he brings the Eucharist to an ill person's bedside, reminding everyone present that Christ is the healer.

In public prayer settings, Father Dan prays over people after a spiritual talk given in the presence of the exposed Blessed Sacrament. He encourages people to keep their eyes on Jesus, and open their hearts to the Lord in prayer as they adore Him in the Eucharist.

Father Dan himself spends many nights and early mornings in prayer in front of the Blessed Sacrament. Gently he encourages his brother priests to do the same as a way to strengthen their relationship with Christ and ultimately strengthen their priesthood and their parishes.

'ONE SOUL AT A TIME'

Father Dan's healing ministry is just one small part of his larger mission to bring souls to Christ as a parish priest –

work which includes visiting the sick; administering the Sacraments; guiding his flock toward the truth of the faith, and searching for lost souls in need of conversion. Leah Moss, a women's ministry volunteer at Father Dan's current parish, said, "Everything he does is for lasting conversion, connecting and pointing souls toward the love of the Heavenly Father."

Laura Warlitner said if he discovers someone has fallen away from the faith, he immediately begins thinking of ways to help them reconnect, and use their talents to serve the Church. "If they like to cook, he'll invite them to join the bereavement committee, or ask them to cook for the priests for the parish penance service. If they like to shop, he'll ask them to buy candy every week for the parish office candy jar. Whatever it takes. He doesn't miss a beat," she said.

Father Dan's inspiration to reach lapsed Catholics and unbelievers comes from the time he spent away from God in his teenage years and early adulthood before settling down enough to hear God's call. At a bar one night with friends, Father Dan made a bet that he would attend Mass every day during Lent. Grace poured into his life during those next 40 days, and instead of going to law school like he planned, he entered the seminary.

Father Dan, the youngest of six children raised in a loving Catholic home, said, "My dad would always say, 'Reach out to those who have fallen away. Bring them back, because that person represents a generation.' If that Catholic heals, then his children will heal, and they pass on that healing one after the other."

The priest says his ministry is "one soul at a time," and he encourages people who have come back to Christ through his efforts to "bring me another you," or "pay it forward."

"Don't just rest on your laurels and soak up all the graces. God has healed you, so bring Him another soul who is in need of healing," he said.

HOPE FOR A MOTHER

This dedication to serving his sick parishioners – no matter when or where – was the difference between life and death for Michelle Maresch.

Four months pregnant with her fifth child, Michelle noticed some unusual spotting. She decided to go to her trusted OB/GYN, Dr. John Bruchalski, founder of the pro-life, missionary-focused Tepeyac Family Center in Virginia.

When she asked him what could have caused the bleeding, he said he needed to take a sonogram. Afterward, he told her some of the worst news a mother could hear – her baby boy was dead.

She drove home alone, tears streaming down her face, wondering how she would tell her husband, Steve, and their four daughters. Later, Michelle and her husband agreed that they wanted to give the baby a funeral even though they didn't know how they would afford it.

It was 1998, just as Lent was beginning, when Michelle went back to the doctor for a D&C procedure to remove the baby because she was so far along in the pregnancy. Everything went smoothly during the procedure, but about an hour after she returned home Michelle began hemorrhaging at an alarming rate.

She arrived back at the hospital in a critical state, requiring emergency surgery because she was in a state of shock, and her blood wouldn't clot. The doctors operating on her couldn't stop the bleeding.

Dr. Bruchalski, remembering the situation, said, "There was a torrent of blood the diameter of a hose ... her life was literally passing from her."

Medically, the team of nurses and doctors were doing everything in their power to save her life, but she was growing paler by the minute, her vital signs waning. Doctors told her husband to quickly call her family and a priest, because she could be paralyzed or dead by the time the bleeding stopped.

"We transfused many platelets and clotting factors ... but once blood becomes thin it takes a lot of help to get it back on board," Dr. Bruchalski said. Michelle also underwent a hysterectomy that night.

GOD'S PLAN

When Father Dan Leary arrived, he walked into the tense, bustling operating room praying quietly. He held the Eucharist in front of himself, and gave Michelle the last rites. After a few minutes, the priest left to pray with Michelle's family, but the life-giving effects of Jesus in the Eucharist were immediately apparent.

"Everything inside the room changed, and she made an abrupt turn for the better. As Father left, the bleeding began to clot and her vital signs began to improve," Dr. Bruchalski said.

"It felt like we were in a sinking boat in the middle of the storm, but the boat that was sinking was actually a patient dying. It was as if the presence of Christ in the Eucharist entered or awoken the boat and the storm subsided," he said.

About an hour after the surgery, Michelle was talking with doctors – she had no lasting effects from the trauma.

Reflecting on what happened, Dr. Bruchalski said he believes God honors Father Dan's deep trust in Jesus' Real Presence in the Eucharist by literally "passing in our midst" and healing people.

God also gave Michelle a gift on the first day she was recovering in the Intensive Care Unit. The nurse who took care of her glowed from head to toe, exuding peace and giving Michelle an overwhelming sense of calm.

Michelle required a wheel chair for three months after the trauma because her body was so weak, and she was anemic for a year.

Michelle said when she showed her general practitioner her medical file he said, "If you had told me this I wouldn't have believed you. People just don't survive that."

From the pathology report taken on Michelle's uterus doctors discovered the cause of the baby's death and the hemorrhaging. In search of nutrients for the baby, the placenta had gone through the uterus, attaching itself to Michelle's other organs.

God required a lot from Michelle during Lent that year, but He also strengthened her with His grace. Michelle always struggled to understand Christ's passion and death on the cross in a personal way, but God used her suffering to help illuminate the mystery for her.

"The Scripture says we are to be Christ's light, we are to be His imitators. We can't say, "I am going to imitate You in Your ministry, I am going to imitate You in Your resurrection, but I am not going to participate in Your passion. The passion completes it all," she said.

Michelle reflects on her journey of faith, and the loss of her son, and sees God's providential hand everywhere.

"There are days that I couldn't even stand, but it's ok ... Because whatever journey, whatever path He has you on, whatever love story He is writing in your hearts – no matter how painful, or how happy it is – it's ok because He gives us everything we need to make it through," she said.

Michelle believes God put Father Dan on her path for a reason.

"Could God have healed me another way? Absolutely. But there is a reason He chooses people. There is a reason He does it a certain way. He chose Father to be the instrument, and if Father had said, 'No,' where would I be?"

Father Dan was quick to give the glory to God, Michelle added.

After Mass one day he stopped Michelle's mother and said, "'This was a Eucharistic miracle ... you have to tell them what Jesus did!'" Michelle said. "There was nothing about it that said, 'Look at me,' it was all about 'Look at Him.'"

Michelle and many people who know Father Dan say he has a palpable zeal for sharing the faith that hasn't dulled since his ordination, but has grown stronger.

GUADALUPE PRAYER

Aileen Vasquez felt blessed to know Father Dan when her 10-month-old son, Joseph, was diagnosed with testicular cancer.

Doctors were surgically repairing what they thought was a hernia when they discovered the tumor. They later biopsed it and removed the testicle with the cancerous tumor.

Doctors strongly suggested radiation and chemotherapy because the surgery carried the risk of contamination of cancer cells to other parts of the body.

They gave Aileen, newly pregnant with her fourth child, a 30-page packet detailing the temporary and permanent side affects of the treatment on a baby. Some of the potential side affects included weight loss, hearing problems, low bone density, and impaired functioning of the kidneys, livers, and eyes.

"It kind of felt like my child could die trying to cure this cancer," she said.

At the time of the diagnosis, Father Dan was leading a pilgrimage to the Shrine of Our Lady of Guadalupe in Mexico. He called Aileen from Mexico when he heard the news. He told her he would go to the Shrine that night, pray for Joseph and write a prayer for him.

The next day, he called her back and dictated the prayer to her. He asked her to make prayer cards using the prayer he gave her and send out emails asking everyone she knew to pray for Joseph.

"The response was incredible. People that I hardly knew and people I didn't know were praying for him," Aileen said.

"There were even people writing from the Philippines and people from across the country."

When Father Dan returned from the pilgrimage he asked Aileen to come to the church so he could pray over the baby. He held the Blessed Sacrament close to the baby and said, "You healed so many in the Scriptures, heal this boy."

After that prayer, Aileen's husband, Michael, felt strongly that the baby was completely healed. Aileen struggled to believe this, but ultimately told doctors they were not going to proceed with the risky radiation and chemotherapy.

Joseph is now 9 years old. His cancer never spread or returned.

"Through the Eucharist, Christ can reach out and touch people and heal them," Aileen said.

REFRESHMENT FOR A THIRSTY SOUL

In 2001, Anna Garcia (name changed to protect anonymity) started having unusual symptoms. She couldn't sleep, and she had difficult menstrual periods, anemia, headaches, and weakness.

Anna, a dentist, imagined the worst and went to see a specialist who diagnosed her with benign uterine tumors that would eventually require surgical removal. Uneasy about surgery, Anna hoped to prolong it as much as possible and she took many different medicines, including alternative medicines, hoping she would heal.

When her body didn't respond, Anna underwent a minor procedure to decrease the size of the tumors, but it didn't cure her painful symptoms.

A few months later, her doctor surgically removed part of the largest tumor, and explained she would need another minor surgery to remove the rest. Anna began imagining grim possibilities even though she knew this was another low-risk surgery. To find peace, she decided to go to Confession.

When Anna expressed her fears to Father Dan in the Confessional she remembers him saying he didn't know what God wanted from her, but he encouraged her to offer her pain and suffering to the Lord.

On the day of the surgery Anna went to Mass and asked God to help her accept His will with the grace she received from the Eucharist.

The surgery did not go as planned. Doctors found a much larger tumor than they expected and, instead of it taking 30 minutes, the surgery lasted four hours.

The next day, Anna became very ill with a high fever, and she returned to the hospital for blood work. The results showed that she had an infection, likely caused by something that happened during the operation. Anna's body soon went into shock because of the bacteria in her bloodstream.

"As a wife and mother my first thoughts included my kids and husband, and all the pain and suffering this was going to cause them. I was scared and feared this was God's will for me," Anna said.

Later that morning doctors told Anna she needed an emergency hysterectomy because the uterus was the source of the infection, but they couldn't proceed with it until the infection was under control.

For an entire day Anna, plagued with constant aches and chills, had no food or water so doctors could perform more tests.

"I was really thirsty and they wouldn't even give me water to refresh my lips," she said. "As my physical situation got worse and worse my spiritual side began to call me and I knew I needed to strengthen it through the blessed rosary ... I reflected upon Christ's suffering during His passion on the cross. All the pain and thirst He suffered from I began to feel."

Because a priest and a sister had already come to pray with Anna, she wasn't expecting any more visitors. She was surprised when Father Dan walked into her room that evening. Anna, her husband and a friend received the Eucharist and then Father Dan gave her the Anointing of the Sick.

Before he left, Father Dan kneeled at her side, taking her hand in his, while praying silently. They spent the next five minutes in deep prayer and Anna called upon the Holy Spirit. She began to sweat excessively and asked for something to dry her face.

"I began to feel a sort of spiritual shower, one that was purifying my body, which in words is unexplainable," she said. "I began feeling as if my sweat was taking with it my disease and leaving my body little by little."

Moments after Father Dan's departure Anna felt as if something needed to exit her body, and she headed toward the bathroom but didn't make it in time.

When they called the nurse to explain what happened, Anna felt much better – her fever was gone. She confidently told her husband she wasn't going to need the surgery anymore, because she was cured. Doctors agreed that Anna no longer needed surgery and she was released from the hospital a few days later.

"We immediately saw that God had shown us His glory through our dear priest Father Dan Leary," she said.

THE FUTURE OF A MINISTRY

Father Dan does not readily publicize the healing aspect of his ministry, but remains open to God's voice, trying to discern what is asked of him each day, and praying for the grace to say yes so he can better serve his parish and community.

Reflecting on the essence of his priestly vocation, Father Dan is reminded of the prayer he chose to place on his ordination card on the day he became a priest and God mystically transformed him – and all other priests before and after him – to continue God's work on earth by acting in Persona Christi:

"Thou Art a Priest Forever"
"To live in the midst of the world,
Without wishing its pleasures;
To be a member of each family,
Yet belonging to none;
To share all sufferings;
To penetrate all secrets;
To heal all wounds;
To go from men to God
And offer Him their Prayers;
To return from God to men
To bring pardon and hope;
To have a heart of fire for charity
And a heart of bronze for chastity;

To teach and to pardon,
Console and bless always –
What a glorious life!
And it is yours, O Priest of Jesus Christ!"

Father Dan believes praying over the sick, just as Jesus and his apostles did, naturally fits in with this description of a priest's vocation. The pastor – aware of the lack of understanding among Catholics about healing charisms – encourages the faithful to let go of their inhibitions and give God's healing power a chance to change their lives.

Father Dan says as long as he knows that doing the work of Christ requires him to have compassion for broken souls and wounded bodies, he will continue offering himself as an empty vessel who gives all the glory back to God.

For more information on Father Dan Leary and the dates and times of his monthly healing Masses please go to www.standrewapostle.org and check the bulletin.

Joseph Vasquez interacts with a nurse during a hospital visit when he was 10-months-old and sick with testicular cancer. Joseph is now a healthy 8-year-old with six brothers and sisters. (Photo Courtesy of Aileen Vasquez)

Father Dan celebrates Mass in front of an image of Our Lady of Guadalupe. The priest said after a visit to the Shrine of Our Lady of Guadalupe in Mexico his healing charism was more fully revealed. (Photo Courtesy of Laura Warlitner)

Father Dan Leary elevates the Eucharist. Many of the miracles connected to this parish priest involve Father Dan's trust in the healing power of Jesus in the Eucharist.
(Photo Courtesy of Laura Warlitner)

ABOUT THE AUTHOR

Laura Wright lives in Poolesville, Md. with her husband, Rob, and their three children. Before starting a family she worked as a reporter for the *Catholic Standard* newspaper in Washington, D.C. She enjoys writing and blogging about faith and family life at www.graceandcookies.net. Go to www. chosentoheal.com for more information on the book and to share stories of God's love and healing.

Made in the USA
Middletown, DE
08 July 2015